Rescue of the Helena Survivors in World War II
A Tale of Incredible Courage

Robert J. Richey

authorHOUSE®

AuthorHouse™
1663 Liberty Drive
Bloomington, IN 47403
www.authorhouse.com
Phone: 1-800-839-8640
This book is a true story. The events actually happened.

First published by AuthorHouse 11/8/2011

ISBN: 978-1-4670-3857-7 (sc)
ISBN: 978-1-4670-3855-3 (hc)
ISBN: 978-1-4685-0199-5 (e)

Library of Congress Control Number: 2011917119

Printed in the United States of America

Contents

FOREWORD

There is a temptation in life when things go badly to lose faith in other individuals around us. Quite often each of us forgets that there are kind, caring people in this world that are always willing to help others in times of distress.

And then again there have been situations or circumstances in the past when individual, or groups of individuals, have faced great danger, in aiding others in trying circumstances.

One perceptive individual once said, "Courage or bravery is not necessarily acting from a lack of fear, but rather in surmounting one's own fears in a worthy cause."

In the past such instances have differed drastically in the circumstances in which others have conducted themselves in the most exemplary manner. However, the actions taken, serve as an inspiration to all of us.

A Poet once wrote:
"The Spring shower that quenches the thirst of a parched land is like unto to each of us when a stranger offers us a helping hand."

OTHER BOOKS BY THIS AUTHOR

(Publisher Authorhouse)
Take Time to Smell the Roses Book of Poetry
ISBN # 1-0433-4472-8 (Paperback)
ISBN # 1-4033-8753-2 (Hardcover)
The Golden Knight Book of Chess The Art of Sacrifice
ISBN # 1-4208-6573-0 (Paperback: Text in Black & White)
Life on the Diamond Bar Ranch A Tale of the West
ISBN # 978-1-4259-6451-1 (Paperback 6" x 9")
Robinhood of the Underworld Dominic Capizzi
ISBN # 978-1-4343-1949-4 (Paperback)
Life on the Diamond Bar Ranch a Tale of the West
ISBN # 1-4259-2982-6(sc) (Text & Pictures in color: 8 ½" x 11")
The Unlikely Hero a Tale of the Sea
ISBN # 978-1-4343-9892-5 (Hardcover)
Mutiny in the United States Navy in World War II A True Story
ISBN # 978-1-4389-6047-0 (Paperback)
ISBN # 978-1-4389-6048-7 (Hardcover)
Destroyer Squadron 12 in the Solomon's Campaign
The Tip of the Lance
ISBN # 978-1-4490-5268-3 (sc)
Blitz Chess Puzzles The Art of Sacrifice
ISBN# 978-1-4520-4798-0 (e) Kindl Version
ISBN # 978-1-4520-4797-3 (sc)
Key Chess Puzzles Sacrificial Chess
ISBN # 978-1-4520-8753-5 (sc)
ISBN # 978-1-4520-8754-2 (e) Kindl Version

My Brother Glenn A Prisoner of the Gestapo *
*German Secret Police
ISBN # 978-1-4567-6687-0 (sc)
ISBN # 978-1-4567-0688-7 (e) Kindl Version
Other Books in Process
2. How Japan Could Have Ruled the Pacific in 1939
A Tale of Treachery & Deceit

PRIMARY FOCUS OF THE BOOK

This book is primarily written about a Light Cruiser in the United States Navy in the year 1943. At about one o'clock in the morning of July 10th the **Helena** took a torpedo that sheared off her bow. Almost immediately two more torpedoes struck her and put her on the bottom. 168 of her crew perished in the sinking. Two destroyers, escorting the **Helena**, rescued as many of the 900 members of the original crew that were in the water that they were able to. 275 survivors however were left; seemingly to their fate. This book is the story of the gallant rescue of these 275 survivors. Other information is included as a lead into the Story of the rescue of the **Helena's** Survivors. It is a tale of incredible courage and valor. It was an example of the American fighting men at their finest.

The following is a few stories about people; many times just ordinary people, who performed heroic deeds, in helping others in peril:

Incident #1

The Attempted Rescue of
Kathy Fiscus

In the afternoon of April 8, 1949, on a Friday, two young girls, and their cousin Gus, were playing in a field located in the city of San Marino. The two girls were sisters. Their names were Kathy and Barbara. Kathy was born on August 21, 1945. On this fateful day she was only 3 years, 8 months and 13 days old.

Nearby was an old abandoned water well that was open. It was 14 inches in diameter. Kathy fell into that well.

Ironically her father, David Fiscus, worked for the California Water & Telephone Company. He had supervised the drilling of this particular well in 1903. He had recently testified before the state legislature about the passage of a proposed law that would require the cementing of all old abandoned wells. But he did not personally see that this particular well, near where he lived, had been sealed.

Within just a matter of hours, a major rescue effort was underway. Total strangers, as well as friends and acquaintances brought drills, derricks, bulldozers and trucks to the site of the tragedy. These volunteers came from a dozen or more towns; some from far away. Three giant cranes were brought along with some 50 powerful searchlights so the rescue effort could be conducted around the clock. The searchlights were provided by Hollywood Studios.

The crew performing the rescue dug down a hundred feet. Kathy was reached that Sunday Night, the third day after the accident. By then at least 10,000 spectators were on the scene standing vigil day and night.

A Doctor was lowered head first into the rescue shaft. When the Doctor reached her, unfortunately he found out that she had died. It was

1

believed that she died shortly after falling in the well, due to a lack of oxygen.

It was truly sad that Kathy was not rescued alive, but still the kindness and help rendered in trying to save her was uplifting. At the time news on radio and television was somewhat new. The News concerning the event received wide coverage.

The exact location of the well is uncertain but the approximate location is known.

Kathy was buried at Glen Abbey Memorial Park in Bonita, California. The inscription on her marker reads, "One Little Girl Who United the World For A Moment."

It is such Acts of Selflessness that aids in buoying up our own spirits at the times in life when we too are being tested.

Incident #2

The Rescue of Jessica Morales

The second incident occurred on October 14, 1987 in Midland, Texas. A baby by the name of Jessica Morales age 6 months, 19 days of age fell down an open well. The well had a very small diameter.

Rescue worker worked for 58 hours from October 14 to October 16 in the rescue effort. The story of the rescue effort gained world wide coverage. Later a movie was produced about the rescue effort.

In this rescue effort a new technology of water jet cutting was utilized. It is puzzling how the effort did not result in the drowning of the baby.

The tragedy received such wide coverage that even President (at the time) Reagan commented, "Everybody in America became godfathers and godmothers of Jessica while this was going on."

The photograph of her being rescued received the 1988 Pulitzer Prize for spot news photography to Scott Shaw of the October American publication.

As part of the rescue effort a man by the name of Ron Short offered to help in the rescue. This man was very muscular and had been born with a birth defect. As a result of this defect he could dislocate both collar bones. His offer was accepted, but he was not involved in the actual rescue.

Although she was rescued alive and in a good condition overall; she still had to have part of one foot amputated, due to loss of circulation while in the well pipe. She graduated some years later from Greenwood High School, near Midland, in May 2004.

The wonderful part of this story is that Jessica was rescued alive and was able to get on with her life. The wonderful individuals who rescued her demonstrated the highest devotion.

Unfortunately, the two men who contributed the most to her rescue did not fare so well. Paramedic Robert O'Donnel in 1995, five years after the event, was found to be suffering from post traumatic stress disorder. He took his own life in 2004.

The other individual, Police Officer William Glasscock, jr., was sentenced to 15 years in prison for various criminal activities. But one must still admire their courage and dedication in helping to rescue a helpless baby at the bottom of a well.

INCIDENT #3

THE ANGEL OF MERCY IN THE ME-109

This incident involved a B-17 bomber in the American Air Force in the Air War over Germany in World War II.

This bomber had been on a bombing raid and had been hit repeatedly by flak and shells from enemy fighters. The Plane dubbed "Ye Olde Pub" (all planes had names) was in terrible shape. The nose of the plane had been blown off; one propeller was gone out of the total of four; the rudder and tail section were shredded, with parts missing. The fuselage had many, many holes in it. The Compass was damaged and useless. Without the compass the pilot had no information as to which way to fly to get back to the Base in England.

The gunner in the top bubble had been blasted all over the top of the plane. Several other crew members were wounded and there was blood all over the inside of the fuselage.

The pilot was a 21 year old man by the name of Charlie Brown and he was attached to the 379th Air Bomber Group based at Kimbolton, England.

The bomber had just flown over a German Fighter Base and Charlie said later, "That his heart sank at the thought."

A German Fighter Pilot at the airfield was ordered to take off and shoot the American Bomber out of the sky. He took off and quickly overtook the bomber. Later in life this pilot, Franz Stigler, stated that when he pulled up near the bomber he was shocked at its condition. Despite having sufficient ammunition to shoot down the helpless bomber, instead he flew alongside and looked at the American Pilot. Charlie was frightened as he expected to suddenly be shot out of the sky, meanwhile trying to fly the heavily damaged bomber.

The German pilot realized that the pilot of the American bomber had no idea as to where he was or which direction England was. Franz, who was flying a ME-109 fighter, instead, waved at the American pilot and directed him to turn 180 degrees and headed him on the way back to England. Franz escorted and guided the stricken plane to and slightly over the North Sea towards England. He then saluted Charlie and turned away to return to his base in Germany.

When Franz returned to his Base he informed his Superior Officer that he had shot down the American bomber over the North Sea.

More than 40 years later, Charlie Brown decided that he wanted to find the Luftwaffe pilot who had compassion on him and his crew. Meanwhile Franz had never confided in any one in the German military, even at Fighter Pilot Reunions, about not shooting down the B-17.

Charlie and four other members of the bomber crew met at the 379th Bomber Group reunion in 1989, all because Franz on that fateful day many years ago had mercy on a wounded foe.

After the war, Charlie remained in the Air Force. He served in many capacities and retired in 1972 as a Lieutenant Colonel. He settled in Miami as head of a Combustion research company.

But over the years the memory of that fateful day that the German Pilot had not shot him and his crew down, haunted him. He was determined to locate the German Pilot.

He wrote numerous letters of inquiry to German military sources with little success. Finally, a notice in a newsletter for former Luftwaffe pilots elicited a response from Franz Stigler. Franz was a German fighter Ace credited with destroying over two dozen Allied planes. It turned out that he was the Angel of Mercy that fateful day just before Christmas in 1943.

Forty six years had passed by the time Charlie found the mysterious man in the ME-109.

Stigler had emigrated to Canada, and was living in Vancouver, British Columbia. After an exchange of letters, Brown flew there for a reunion. The two men visited each other several times and appeared jointly before Canadian and American military audiences. Their most recent appearance was at the Air Force Ball in Miami in September 1995, where the former foes were honored.

In his first letter to Brown, Stigler wrote, "All of these years, I have wondered what happened to the B-17. Did she make it or not?"

Brown responded, "Just barely."

When asked later why Franz had not shot down the bomber he was quoted as saying, "I didn't have the heart to finish off those brave men." Later Stigler said also, "I flew alongside them for a long time. They were desperately trying to get home and I was going to let them do that. I could not have shot them down. It would have been the same as shooting at a man in a parachute."

Franz Stigler passed away on March 22, 2008. May God rest his Soul!

INCIDENT #4

A KIND FRENCH FAMILY

My brother Thomas Glenn Richey was a Waist Gunner in a B-17 in the Eighth Air Force involved in the Air War over Germany in 1944. On his 22nd mission his plane lost an engine. The pilot jettisoned his bombs and dropped down to tree tops to get away from the enemy fighters.

On that day, June 4, 1944, just a couple of days before D-day (The American, British and Canadian Invasion of Fortress Europe) my brother's bomber was hit by antiaircraft fire just inside Dieppe. Dieppe is just inside the French coast. There was a Canadian Commando raid on Dieppe earlier that ended in disaster.

The antiaircraft fire from a battery of German 88's heavily damaged the bomber. The Pilot was killed and the Co-pilot put the plane on Automatic pilot and bailed out. The tail gunner was killed along with the ball turret gunner. There were only three men of the crew of nine still alive.

My brother was the last man alive aboard. He stood there in the waist debating about trying to fly the plane out over the channel near England and bailing out. This way he could hope to be rescued. He could see England in the distance across the Channel. While he was debating the plane hit a big air pocket. When the plane lunged it threw him out the hatch. One foot caught in the hatch hinge. In desperation he pulled the parachute cord. The shock from the chute opening pulled his boot out the hatch hinge. He landed in a farming area.

He gathered up his chute and hobbled over to the nearest farm house. The kind French family that lived there took him in. They took care of his badly injured ankle, and fed him. Then they hid him from any enemy that might be lurking in the vicinity.

It was the Mayor of the nearby community of Embruelle who took my brother in and provided him with food, clothing and shelter.

Later when his hair had grown out he was given a French haircut. He was wearing French clothing when he was then transported to Paris. It was hoped he would be secreted out of France, but he was apprehended in Paris by the Gestapo.

Since he was out of uniform he was put in the death camp at Buchenwald (One of the worst concentration camps). Later for some unknown reason he was transferred to Stalag Luft 3 (a prison camp for Air Force Personnel).

Over a period of months in captivity he went from about 165 lbs. down to less than a 100 lbs. Most of the American prisoners died.

He was released by elements of General George Patton's Third Army and returned home.

He regained most of his health and lived to be in his 80's and was able to see his family again.

But we can all admire the French people who helped in his time of trouble. They risked their very lives in helping downed Fliers. If they had been apprehended they would have been shot.

My brother related how he had been tortured and beaten by the Germans, who were trying to get information from him as to the names of the French people who had helped him. But, he never did tell them.

Later my brother and his family received several letters from the French family that helped him. Copies of these letters follow:

Letter #1

Dear Friend:

Since you are gone away, we have often thought of you and of your friend. Many events are arrived for that time where we went up to see you to Embreville to Mr. Remy's.

The Boches are away, and we are very quiet. We heard them, during the last nights, passing before our house and shouting. They were pushing little babies-coaches, wheel-barrows, arms-coaches. They had no horses, some farmers of the neighbourhood with their own carriages and horses went to accompany them to half-road. Sometimes, they sung, but it was not a glad song, but a sad one.

I am surely late, and when you receive my letter, it will be too late, but I wish you a happy New Year, a good health and your next coming back home. I hope see you again after the war, you will come in a plane and we shall spend pleasant days together.

An American plane has landed about to three miles from here. It is not smashed like yours. It is a fortress with four motors. I have not yet been and see it. The weather was too rainy and on the earth, was snow.

I always play music, but no much. I have too much work: English, German, Latin, Mathematics and so on.

Today, Friday, I stay home. I am a little ill. My parents and my sister are well, I hope you are the same.

I hope to receive your news, and waiting this day, I send you my best memorial.

Your respectful friend,

Renne

Renne Veloison
Beauchauefe,
Somme

France

Letter #2

I am sending some of our news. We have been liberated since Sept. 2. We saved the life of our friend Thomas Richey. My husband ran down the field when he heard the plane fall so you would not be a prisoner.

I remember when my husband brought you back to the house and your leg was hurt. I took care of you and the Dr. came to see you. You were so sick and you were white. It is a strange life to be an aviator. Your friend that fell at Embreuelle, I hope you went back together. We came back to get you at 6 o'clock that night, you were white as a sheet. You were wondering where you would be. You went to the mayor at Embreuelle who fed you. For ourself we are only working people and we were afraid to keep you because some one might tell and the Germans would get you.

My children talk about you often. They remember when you were on the bed in the bedroom upstairs. You were not the only one I have saved and I keep lots of young men that were with the under ground. Do you remember the one that talked to you in English. We are good French people and we are to receive medals for the service we give. Now the address of your friend that came down in the parachute. I hope his family knows about him since I gave you the address. Today I am in the modd to write. I will write to some English and Canadians. I saved their lives too. My Dear Friend, I saved your life on June 5. The day before D-Day. I will have no more to tell you except to tell about Gen. DeGaulle in France. Our good chief all ways worked for us.

My husband and my three children send our love.

Your Good Friend of France.

11

Letter #3

I am sending some of our news. We have been liberated since
Sept. 2. We saved the life of our friend Thomas Richey. My
husband ran down the field when he heard the plane fall so
you would not be a prisoner.

I remember when my husband brought you back to the house and
your leg was hurt. I took care of you and the Dr. came to
see you. You were so sick and you were white. It is a
strange life to be an aviator. Your friend that fell at
Embreuelle, I hope you went back together. We came back
to get you at 8 o'clock that night, you were white as a
sheet. You were wondering where you would be. You went
to the mayor at Embreuelle who fed you. For ourself we
are only working people and we were afraid to keep you
because some one might tell and the Germans would get you.

My children talk about you often. They remember when you
were on the bed in the bedroom upstairs. You were not the
only one I have saved and I keep lots of young men that
were with the under ground. Do you remember the one that
talked to you in English. We are good French people and
we are to receive medals for the service we give. Now the
address of your friend that came down in the parachute. I
hope his family knows about him since I gave you the address.
Today I am in the modd to write. I will write to some English
and Canadians. I saved their lives too. My Dear Friend, I
saved your life on June 5. The day before D-Day. I will
have no more to tell you except to tell about Gen. DeGaulle
in France. Our good chief all ways worked for us.

My husband and my three children send our love.

                                    Your Good Friend of France.

Incident #4

The Kindness of a Truck Driver

This writer could almost write a book about the kindness others have shone to him and others, but time and space is limited.

In the Fall of 1947 this writer drove his wife and young son of 2 or 3 years of age from the Gulf Coast up to South Dakota. This was only a couple of years after the end of World War II. Times were very difficult for young Service Men just out of the military.

The car we were in was an old Hudson Terraplane that had, had many miles of travel. It was in bad shape, but was all that this writer could afford at the time.

On the return trip back to Texas, while in Indiana, the car broke down. The universal joint separated and the transmission caught fire.

A kindly Truck Driver stopped and helped put out the fire. He then drove us to a nearby Wrecking Yard and Repair Facility of a friend of his.

This owner's wife helped in feeding my young son while the Owner helped me repair the car. The transmission had to be taken off; cleaned up and reinstalled. New gaskets and a new Universal Joint were also required. Grease was also included.

When asked what he was owed he said, "You do not owe me anything." That happened many years ago but this writer has never forgotten the kindness and consideration that this man and his wife extended to two strangers in distress.

Incident #5

The Japanese 442ND Regimental Combat Team

It would be impossible to pass up this one more incident. After the attack on Pearl Harbor most Americans were very angry at the Japanese.

In fact this anger spilled over to Japanese who were citizens in this country.

By Executive Order all Japanese residing on the Western Seaboard were taken and transported to Relocation Camps further back from the west coast. These Camps were bordered by barbwire and had armed guards around them.

After the Attack on Pearl Harbor all young Japanese males in this country were classified as 4C (enemy aliens) and were exempt from the Draft.

On February 19, 1941 President Franklin D. Roosevelt signed Executive Order 9066, authorizing military authorities "to prescribe military areas in such places and of such extent as he or the approximate Military Commander may determine, from which any or all persons may be excluded, and with respect to which, the right of any person to enter, remain in, or leave shall be subject to whatever restrictions the Secretary of War or the appropriate Military Commander may impose in his discretion." Although the ethnic background of those subject to this order did not specifically identify those affected; it was obvious it was directed almost solely at the Japanese who were American citizens.

108 military proclamations were issued which resulted in the incarceration of 110,000 people of Japanese ancestry.

Hawaii had a large population of Japanese (150,000 out of a total of

400,000). Since interment was not practical. Military Law was established instead.

The removal of all Japanese from active military service in early 1942 was not felt to be practical. However, More Japanese American soldiers of the 298th and 299th Infantry regiments of the Hawaii' National Guard were kept in service.

A surprising thing happened, in that the discharged members of the Hawaii Territorial Guard petitioned General Emmons to allow them to assist in the war effort. The petition was granted, and they formed a group called the Varsity Victory Volunteers which performed various construction jobs for the military.

Because of Security concerns in the event of a Japanese Invasion the Battalion was set sail for Oakland, California on June 10, 1942. From there they were ordered to Camp McCoy located in Wisconsin. The Battalion was re-designated the 100th Infantry Battalion and was nicknamed the Puka, Puka Division.

The men in this Battalion performed so well in training that on February 1, 1943 the government reversed its earlier decision and approved the formation of a Japanese Combat Unit. Each member was required to take an Oath of Allegiance.

The Oath read, "Are you willing to serve in the armed forces of the United States on combat duty, wherever ordered?" "Will you swear unqualified allegiance to the United States of America and faithfully defend the United States from any or all attacks by foreign or domestic forces, and forswear any form of allegiance or obedience to the Japanese Emperor, or any other foreign government, power or organization?"

Nearly a quarter of the Nisei young males answered "no" to swearing to the oath. However, more than 75% indicated that they were willing to enlist in the US armed forces (although not all of them actually did).

The Army called for 1,500 volunteers from Hawaii and 3,000 from the mainland. An overwhelming number of the 10,000 were from the Islands. The Army request for volunteers was less enthusiastically received by the mainland young Japanese males. There was a feeling of resentment because of their families being confined in the Camps.

In all, the final group of volunteers numbered 3,000 from the islands and 800 from the mainland. This group of volunteers were designated the 442nd Infantry Regimental Combat Team. Their motto became "The Go For Broke regiment". These men had the famous saying that, "Americanism is not, and never will be, a matter of race or ancestry".

At full strength this Combat Team consisted of three infantry battalions. After training was completed, the Combat Team was landed at Oran in Algeria and was scheduled to guard supply trains in North Africa.

The new Commanding Officer insisted that this group be given Combat Assignments and it was attached to the US 34th Infantry Division.

After fighting was concluded successfully in North Africa, the Combat Team was landed in Italy and took part in Combat in that theatre.

After other action in Italy, the 442nd continued in the push up Italy and was attached to the 88th Infantry Division. They participated in the fight to liberate Bruyeres.

Next they were attached to the 36th Infantry Division that was originally a Texas National Guard Unit. This group of Texans were cut off and surrounded by Germans. The 442nd broke through the German lines and rescued the group of soldiers from Texas. Over a five day period of fighting from October 26 to October 30, 1944 the 442nd suffered the loss of nearly half of its roster in the fighting. There were over 800 casualties, including 121 dead. They rescued 211 members of the 36th Infantry Division's 1st Battalion, 141st Infantry. Those rescued had been surrounded in the Vosges Mountains.

The paradox is that many of these men of Japanese ancestry, whose families had been confined in prison camps, were able to put their, perhaps justified resentments aside, and risk their lives to help out soldiers of a completely different ethnic background.

This merely goes to bear out the motto of the members of the 442nd that, "Americanism is not, and never will be, a matter of race or ancestry".

Incidentally members of the 442nd suffered a casualty rate of 314 percent; received 9,486 purple hearts for wounds received, divided by some 3,000 in-theatre personnel. US Army battle reports show the official casualty rate, combining KIA (killed) and WIA (wounded and missing) totals, 93%, which was still uncommonly high.

This truly is a story of uncommon valor.

INCIDENT #6

THE CANDY BOMBER OF WEST BERLIN

After World War II ended the Victorious Western Powers and Russia divided Germany up. Each country then occupied part of Germany. The city of Berlin was totally inside the Russian Sector. The city of Berlin was divided into the Eastern Sector which was controlled by Russia, and the Western Sector of the city which was not.

In the summer of 1948 Russia blocked all railway and roadway access to Berlin to the Western Powers. The only method of transport was by air.

The overall intent of the Blockade by Russia was to threaten the West Berliners with starvation. With the total city dependent on Russia for food and supplies, Russia could control the entire city.

To counter this threat an Airlift was instituted to deliver food and other necessities by air. This effort required a minimum of 4,000 ton of supplies each and every day to be flown from England. The Airlift was conducted by the US Air Force, Royal Air Force and air force planes and crews from other Commonwealth Nations.

This means of supplying Berlin from the air existed from June 24, 1948 to May 12, 1949.

One day one of the American pilots, a Lt. Halvorson was standing by a fence adjacent to the airport, where a large number of ragged little boys were standing on the other side. He talked with them through the fence for at least an hour. He noticed that although they had almost nothing none of them asked for or begged him for anything. They were just watching the planes land and takeoff. The Lt. reached in his pocket and took out two pieces of chewing gum. He handed it through the fence to two of these little boys. As he watched them he noticed the boys did not fight over the gum. Instead each one took his piece of gum and divided it up into tiny pieces so each boy would have a taste. The few that did not get a piece of the gum were instead given a piece of the wrapper to smell.

The Lt. was moved by the plight of so many young boys existing almost on the verge of starvation. After a bit of thought he came up with an idea. He told the little boys, through one who could speak English, that the next time he flew in they should watch for him. He would waggle his wings as he approached the landing site so they would know it was his plane. He would have a surprise for them.

When he got back to his Base in England he went down and bought all of the candy bars at the Base PX. He then scrounged around collecting all of the handkerchiefs he could find. He made a crude parachute out of each handkerchief and tied a candy bar to each one.

On his next flight to Berlin the boys were waiting and watching and he waggled his wings. Then members of his crew threw the chutes, with the candy attached, out the hatch so the boys could retrieve them.

Soon the Lt.'s buddies began to donate their rations of candy and handkerchiefs. The effort began to spread. Word began to appear in the Press about the "Candy Bomber."

When the Colonel in charge of his Unit heard about the Candy Bombing he chewed him out for throwing unauthorized packages out of an Air Force Plane in flight. The General had chewed out the Colonel. But, by then the idea had acquired a life of its own.

On a visit back to the United States, between flights, he happened to be interviewed by a Reporter. During the interview he was asked, "What did he need to continue his popular Candy Bomber Operation?" Jokingly he remarked, "All he needed was a Boxcar full of candy bars."

Shortly after his return to Germany a box car loaded with 3,000 pounds of chocolate bars arrived that were addressed to Uncle Wiggly Wings. It was rumored that a firm by the name of The American Confectioners Association had donated the candy bars.

He began to get letters from other pilots in the Airlift who wanted to join in the Candy Bombing Operation.

Back in the States even school children starting preparing handkerchief parachutes with candy bars attached and forwarded them to the Lt. for delivery by air to the ragged children of West Berlin.

The above story just shows the power of one simple chance kind

act and how it brings out the best in people. It is indeed strange that just two packages of gum started something that could generate so much good will as opposed to the evil intents that the Russians had for Western Berlin.

Incident #7

A Not So Happy Ending

It happened above the airfield on Guadalcanal during the worst part of that life or death struggle between the Japanese and the US Marines.

About the only rest the marines got when they were not in the front lines protecting against a night time assault was at night.

Unfortunately in the middle of the night one lone Japanese plane would fly over the marine encampment. This pilot soon became known to the marines as Washing Machine Charley. The pilot was tuned in to the Marine Radio Fighter Frequency. He would then start taunting them by saying things like, "Come up and fight Yankee Sons of Bitches. Haven't you got any guts etc." This sort of banter really chapped the marines listening to this sort of challenge. After waking all of the men on the ground up, he would fly back and forth like a gnat or a horse fly just pestering them as long as he could. He would keep this kind of hen house stuff up until he began to run low on fuel. The motor of the plane he flew had deliberately been set so that it made a very annoying singsong noise that sounded like a washing machine to the frustrated marines.

The marines had tried to shoot him down more than once, but he was flying too high for the guns to reach him. They had tried to climb up to his elevation to try and get him that way but the marine planes were too heavy to fly that high. This sort of game went on far longer than the marines felt like enduring it.

Finally the airplane mechanics took a plane that had been damaged too much to be used in combat. Then they set about to reduce its weight as much as possible. When they got through that thing was a lot like a glider with a single machine gun up front.

One night when Charlie came over on his nightly visit the marines had a surprise for him. The marine pilot managed to reach Charley's altitude and shot him down.

But in a way it was kind of a shame. According to the records he had never harmed anyone on the ground. The single bombs that he usually dropped just blew up a small patch of the jungle.

If the marine pilot had had the tendency for mercy like the German pilot of the ME-109 perhaps it would have had a more merciful ending. But the marines were not in any jovial mood to be harassed by any of the enemy.

Actually the marine pilot could have flown alongside of him and on the radio said something like, "OK Charlie you have had your fun. Up to now you haven't hurt anyone. Be smart, quit while you are ahead. Any next visit by you could be your last."

But as General Sherman said during the American Civil War, "War is hell."

A Chain of Events

A Long Chain of seemingly unconnected Events lead to the sinking of the USS Helena in Kula Gulf on the night of July 10th 1943.

One such Event was the invention of the Steam Engine. Up to that time Ships were constructed of wood and were propelled by Sails. In earlier days Romans and Greeks had Galleys that were rowed by Slaves chained to the Seats, and pulling long oars. The Norwegian Vikings had long boats that were propelled by their crews using oars and sails. The Chinese used Junks while the men from India used Dhows; a Lanteen type sailing vessel. Egypt has always been a land without significant stands of trees but rather a desert type landscape with stands of Date Palm trees. The Egyptians therefore used boats on the Nile made of reeds, even back in the days of Noah.

The first patent for a crude steam engine was awarded in 1698 to Thomas Savery. Thomas Newcomen improved on Savery's design. But, it wasn't until James Watt improved on the steam engine that it became a truly viable (useable, practicable) piece of machinery. This occurred in the second half of the 18th century and contributed to the advent of the Industrial Revolution.

A steam engine basically uses the energy of steam to operate machinery of different types. When water is heated until it flashes into steam there is an enormous expansion that when contained yields high pressure gases (hydrogen and oxygen in the form of water). Steam is a clean form of energy but it can be an indirect source of pollution when coal is used to heat the water.

The steam engine has found great usage in operating locomotives (until the advent of the diesel engine) and steamships. Nuclear Power Plants have replaced some steam turbines in ships.

With the advent of ships powered by steam, the ships were no longer at the mercy of the vargaries of the wind. Ships no longer had to confine themselves to the Trade Winds. There were times in sailing days when the winds would die down and the ship would be becalmed for days waiting for the winds to freshen and drive them on their way.

ADMIRAL PERRY'S VISIT TO JAPAN JUNE 6, 1853

The incident detailed on the following pages reveals how a chance incident aided in a large measure of bringing Japan out of a primitive isolationist condition. This transformation contributed in an indirect way to the sinking of the US Light Cruiser USS Helena many years later.

In 1852 a Fleet of 15 American Navy ships departed an East Coast port for a voyage around the World and Admiral Perry was in command.

Photo of Admiral Perry

This Fleet consisted of three frigates; the Flagship Mississippi accompanied by the Susquehanna and the Powhatan. All three frigates were of the older fashioned side wheeler steamers like those found on the Mississippi river. They each had hulls constructed of wood. Their boilers were built of quarter inch copper plate which was strong enough to sustain a steam pressure of 8 pounds per square inch. The maximum speed that they could cruise at was 8 knots.

In company with the three cruisers were several sloops of war. These sloops were the Plymouth, Saratoga and several others.

The Flagship Susquehanna accompanied by the Mississippi

In November of 1852 this fleet of ships sailed from Hampton Roads, Virginia. On the voyage they visited Madiera, the Azores and St. Helena. After leaving Cape Town a visit was paid to Mauritius located in the Indian Ocean then they proceeded to Point de Galle and Ceylon. Finally the Fleet arrived at Singapore. After leaving Singapore the next stop was at Hong Kong in China and finally they arrived at Shui in Japan. Shui was the capitol of Lew Chew and the American ships arrived there on June 6, 1853 after a voyage of at least seven months.

At the time Shui was a walled city. Through interpreters Admiral Perry indicated to the Japanese Officials that he and his entourage desired to visit this walled part of the city. He was informed that such a request could not be granted.

Admiral Perry, according to the Records was a head strong man, and informed the Japanese Officials, that he intended to land and visit this part of the city, whether the Officials approved or not. Upon his arrival it became obvious the Japanese were displeased by such lack of International Courtesy, but realizing that the Americans had more military power the gates to the walled city were opened for the Admiral's entourage to enter.

Needless the show of strength of the American delegation of 300 sailors and marines armed with guns, and a dozen howitzers loaded with ammunition, influenced the Japanese to accede to the Admirals demands. The American contingent then, according to the Records, marched arrogantly all around the city.

It is possible this ill advised and unwarranted show of Power may have come back to haunt the United States in later years. Nations and individuals do not easily overlook boorish behavior by other Nationals.

After departing Shui the Fleet of ships visited at the Bay of Yeddo and on to Yokohama. The Bay had never been charted, so the visiting ships had no information as to the depth of the water. Work was begun on performing the charting.

Meanwhile many Japanese, by the hundreds, came to the harbor. They came in boats loaded with men armed with swords, spears, bows and arrows. They were escorted by their lone best ship. It was an old junk; that had only one sail.

While the Flagship of the American Fleet tried to proceed with the charting of the harbor; Japanese in these many small crafts tried to prevent the charting of the harbor. The Americans, according to the records, unwisely used the threat of military force to accomplish their mission. This sort of bullying, undoubtedly led to a mistrust and contempt for Americans, that lingered long after the American ships departed.

It became apparent to the American contingent that although the Japanese were not belligerent, they never the less made it clear that they preferred to be left alone.

However one intriguing thing did take place. Daguerreotype photos were taken of Japanese nationals. They were then shown these photos of themselves. These were the first photos ever taken in Japan.

Also a telegraph line was erected that stretched for 1,200 feet. One end of the line was attached to the Temple and the other end to a hut in the woods. Within 24 hours the Japanese, to the surprise of the Americans, had mastered the ability to operate the system and send and receive messages themselves.

Upon arrival in Japan the Admiral had delivered a personal letter from President Millard Fillmore to the ranking Japanese Official. The sentiments expressed in the letter were not reflected in the actions taken by

Admiral Perry. The President had stressed the desire for the encouragement of establishing Trade Relations between the two countries.

It is reported that Admiral Perry read extensively about Japan before undertaking the voyage. Also, that he published a report on the voyage upon his return to New York, when he arrived back there in 1855. The title of the Report was, "Narrative of the Expedition of an American Squadron to the China Seas and Japan."

Another source of information yields even more disturbing news concerning Admiral Perry's conduct on arrival at Japan. In this report it is reported that he openly threatened the Japanese Authorities with military action if they did not consent to his demands. In fact he had his gun crews fire at some buildings near the harbor to reinforce his threat of military action.

Admiral Perry departed Japan and returned in the year 1854. On this second visit he had twice as many ships. Where the extra ships came from is not explained. However, the Japanese prepared a treaty that the Admiral signed. The treaty complied with all of the demands that President Fillmore had outlined in his letter. This signing of the treaty was titled the Convention of Kanagawa and it was signed on March 31, 1854. Admiral Perry mistakenly believed that the treaty had been prepared and accepted by the Japanese Royalty but this turned out not to be so.

Prior to the visit by Admiral Perry from 1797 to 1809 American ships had traded in Nagasaki under the Dutch flag. The Dutch had requested this as they at the time were in conflict with the British. At the time Japan limited foreign trade to the Dutch and Chinese under the policy they called Sakoku.

Efforts were made by American Representatives in 1837, and in 1846 to establish trade relations with Japan, without success. Finally in 1849 a Commander James Biddle was able to achieve successful negotiations at Nagasaki.

A Photo of Typical US Sailors in
The day of Sailing Ships

Photo # NH 63033   "Ten Old Salts". USS Hartford. 1877

A History of the Ironclads

The next link in the Chain of Events that led to the sinking of the Helena occurred during the American Civil War.

The advances in warship construction that occurred during the Civil War in the United States, led to a worldwide revolution in warship design.

With the introduction of Steam Power for the propulsion of ships of all types led Countries to design a different type of warship.

When the Civil War broke out between the Northern and Southern states in the United States in 1861 the Secretary of the Navy in the south became enthusiastic about the advantages of armor. It is stated that knowing that the Confederacy could not match the North in building ships; another way had to be found to equalize the situation. He came to believe that the South needed to build warships that were armored. A group of men were gathered who shared his vision of constructing an armored warship. John M. Brooke, John Porter and William P. Williamson were three of this group.

After reviewing all of the factories in the south it was found that none of them had the capability of building the engines that were required, certainly not within the existing time frame. The only facility that could meet the requirements would need at least a year to accomplish the task. This factory was the Tredegar Iron Works and it was located in Richmond. Time would not permit that much delay. The North had blockaded the South on the sea and time was critical.

After being confronted with this information Williamson decided that the only practical option was to raise the previously sunken **Merrimac.** It was though that its engines could be refurbished and used in a new ironclad.

Designs for the new warship were prepared on July 11, 1861 and after approval was given the work was started immediately. The burned out hull of the **Merrimac** was raised and towed into the graving dock. The Union

Forces had failed to destroy this dock. During this conversion process the design was modified to include a ram installed at the bow. She was to mount ten guns. There were to be six 9 inch smooth bore Dahlgrens; two 6.4 inch and two 7 inch Brooke rifles. Instead of installing the previously planned one inch thick armor; instead double plates were used each being 2 inches thick. 14 gun ports were included in the design. Four gun ports were to be for broadsides guns with one to Starboard (right side) and the other to the Port (left side).

Changes in design and the inadequate Southern Transportation System led to delays. The ship was not launched until February 3, 1861. The commissioning was not performed until February 17, 1862. The new ship was named the CSS **Virginia.** And the guns that were installed were in a fixed position (i.e. unable to be rotated).

Confederate Ship CSS Virginia

The North's Construction of the USS Monitor

Retaliation by the North further contributed to the sinking of the **Helena** many years later as it led to a world wide ship building frenzy.

The Secretary of the Navy in the North at the time was a Gideon Wells. He waited until Congress could meet so he could get permission to consider building an Ironclad ship to counter the Confederacies ironclad. The ship that was built was the **Virginia.**

Permission was granted on August 3, 1861 and a commission was appointed. This group came to be called the Ironclad Board and it consisted of three senior naval officers. The officers of this Board were to be responsible for selecting the best design from seventeen proposals. Three candidate designs of the seventeen were selected. The first ironclad to be built was the most radical departure from traditional design of the seventeen proposals. The designer was a Swedish engineer by the name of John Ericsson and the new ship was named the **Monitor.**

John Ericsson had a Navy Yard located on the East River in Greenpoint, Brooklyn. The design incorporated many new and impressive features. The most significant features concerned the armor and armament.

A Sketch of The Union Ship USS Monitor

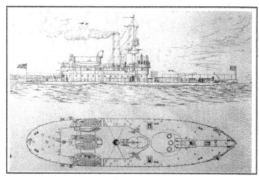

Instead of mounting a large number of guns the **Monitor** would only mount two guns of large caliber. The designer wished to mount two 12 inch guns but had to settle for two 11 inch guns. The two guns were to be mounted in a cylindrical turret. The turret was to be 20 feet in diameter. It was to be 9 feet in height. The turret was to be covered with iron of a thickness of 8 inches. The turret had two guns mounted side by side that were be capable of being rotated. It was to be rotated using a steam engine because of its great weight. However due to the location of a pilot house the guns could not fire straight forward. The turret was isolated and was without entry from inside of the ships hull.

Despite delays in starting construction and the radical design the **Monitor** was completed a few days before the Confederate ship **Virginia**. However, the **Virginia** was placed in active service first.

THE IRONCLADS APPEAR ON THE SCENE

The next link in the chain that eventually led to the dominance of Japan's Navy in 1941 occurred of all places in the United States. At the time of this occurrence the United States was at war with itself. North and South had been locked in the deadly embrace of the Civil War that had erupted in 1861.

The **Virginia** went into battle with the **Monitor** basically without a Captain. The South had a rigid military structure. Although a Lieutenant Roger Jones had overseen the construction he was not allowed to Captain the **Virginia**. The Confederate States Navy had an aggressive officer by the name of Franklin Buchanan. Secretary of State Mallory appointed Buchanan to be flag officer in charge of the defence of the Norfolk area and along the James River. Technically he was in command of the **Virginia** though he was not aboard. Jones was retained aboard but as Executive Officer, second in command. Technically, he was in Command of the **Virginia**.

On the Union side Flag Officer Louis M. Goldsborough was in command of the North Atlantic Blockading Squadron that prevented Southern ships from leaving port. This squadron also prevented ships from any other country from entering any harbor that could serve the South (specifically France).

This officer had devised a plan where his group of frigates would get the **Virginia** in a cross fire. His plans went awry when four of his ships ran aground in the confined shallow waters. Unfortunately (for the North at least) on the day of the battle this officer was not on board his ship.

A Captain John Marston who was on board the USS **Roanoke** was in command of the Union ships which included the **Monitor**. The **Roanoke** was one of the unfortunate ships that had run aground and was stranded. Captain Marston was in no position to have any positive effect in the coming battle. He was basically relegated to the sidelines.

In this situation the captain John L. Worden of the **Monitor** contributed the most to the outcome of the battle.

THE BATTLE BETWEEN THE VIRGINIA
AND THE MONITOR

The battle was joined in Hampton Roads on March 8, 1862, the second year of the Civil War. The **Virginia** steamed into Hampton Roads accompanied by the **Raleigh** and **Beaufort** and was joined by the James **River Squadron which consisted of the Patrick Henry, Jamestown** and the **Teaser.**

Captain Buchanan had intentionally misled all the members of his group of ships by letting them believe that his excursion was just a practice maneuver. It is stated that the crews on his ships suspected that this was the real thing.

As the Confederate ships steamed past a Union Strongpoint at Newport News, a Union gun battery fired on the **Patrick Henry.** The shells temporarily disabled her when a shot struck here boiler. Four of her crew were killed from the shot. After hasty repairs the **Patrick Henry** rejoined the group.

On the first day of the battle the Union forces had five warships in addition to supporting vessels. There was the sloop **Cumberland** at anchor by the frigate **Congress.** The frigate **St. Lawrence** and the steam frigates **Roanoke** and **Minnesota** were at anchor near Fort Monroe.

The latter three Union Ships saw the **Virginia** get underway, but all three soon ran aground and were out of the battle. The **Virginia** headed straight for the Union Squadron.

The battle opened when the Union Tug **Zouave** fired on the **Beaufort.** The gun fire was ineffective (shipboard guns were very short range).

The **Virginia** did not open fire until within easy range of the **Cumberland.** The **Cumberland** and **Congress's** return fire bounced harmlessly from the iron plates of the **Monitor.** However, the noise of the impact of the shots must have stunned the crew of the **Monitor.**

Meanwhile the **Virginia** rammed the **Columbia** below the waterline and sinking her rapidly. According to the Records the **Columbia** continued firing until she sank. 121 of her crew went down with her. Another 39 were wounded but survived.

Unfortunately (for the Confederacy at least) when the **Virginia** rammed the **Columbia** her ram remained joined with the sinking ship and she almost got dragged down also. The Ram broke off saving the **Monitor** but she was now without the ram.

Captain Buchanan next turned **Virginia's** guns on the **Congress**. The Captain of the **Congress** having seen what happened to the **Columbia** and fearing he too would be rammed and sunk intentionally grounded his ship.

Meanwhile the other Confederate ships from the James River Squadron had joined the fight. The Captain of the group a Lieutenant Joseph B. Smith ordered his ships to commence firing on the **Congress**. This unequal battle went on for over an hour until the Captain of the **Congress** ran up the surrender flag.

In the temporary truce that ensued, and survivors were being taken off the **Congress**, a Union Battery on the nearby shore took the **Virginia** under fire. In retaliation the gun crews of the **Virginia** were ordered to resume firing on the **Congress** with hot shot. Near midnight flames reached her ammunition storage areas and she exploded. The dead numbered 110 or missing or presumed drowned while 26 were wounded and survived. 10 of this number died later.

Although the **Virginia** had emerged in better shape she still was not unscathed. Her smokestack had been riddled which reduced her already slow speed, Two of her guns had been put out of action. Several armor plates had been loosened by the impact of the close range shots.

Two of **Virginia's** crew had been killed and seven were wounded. Captain Buchanan was one of the wounded by a rifle shot in the thigh. So it appears that the crews of the ships were also taking potshots at each other with rifles.

At this point in the battle the James River Squadron turned its attention to the Union ship **Minnesota**. This ship had left the vicinity of Fort Monroe and so was not under the protection of the Fort's guns. Meanwhile the Minnesota had also run aground.

The deeper draft of the **Virginia** prevented her from approaching the **Minnesota** close enough to effective fire at her. Darkness had set in, and reduced the effectiveness of the other Confederacy ships from wreaking further damage on the **Minnesota**.

At this point the Southern ships withdrew with the expectations of resuming the battle the following morning. The **Virginia** and her accompanying ships withdrew to the safety of the Confederate waters off Sewell's Point where they anchored for the night.

2ᴺᴰ Day of Battle of the Monitor and Virginia

While the **Virginia** was anchored at night, the wounded were taken ashore and temporary repairs were made. Since Captain Buchanan was wounded, his second in command Executive Officer Roger Jones assumed command. According to the Records Lieutenant Jones was also a very aggressive individual.

While the **Virginia** was making preparations for the next day of battle the **Monitor** was steaming toward the scene of the previous day's battle.

The **Congress** was still burning when the **Monitor** arrived on the scene. The **Monitor** had been rushed there in the hopes of protecting the remaining Union ships and preventing the **Virginia** from bombarding Union cities. Its first assignment was to protect the wounded **Minnesota** so the **Monitor** dropped anchor nearby.

At dawn, the following morning of March 9, 1862 the **Virginia** left her anchorage and moved to attack the **Minnesota** again. Three other ships accompanied her. They found that their path was blocked by the **Monitor**.

Unfortunately the commander of the **Virginia** failed to pay enough attention to the new foe, the **Monitor**. Soon it became apparent that the only recourse was to fight her.

Both ships began to shell each other at close range for hours. Neither one could gain any advantage as the armor of both resisted the opponent's shots.

The commander of the **Virginia**, expecting to fight wooden ships, had available only explosive shells and not armor piercing shells. This was because he had not expected to face another armored vessel.

The 15 pounds of explosives used by the **Monitor's** guns proved to be ineffective in penetrating the armor of the **Virginia**. Later tests revealed the **Monitor's** guns could safely fire a charge of 30 pounds of powder. This would have made the guns able to penetrate the armor of the **Virginia.**

The battle ended when a chance shot struck the pilot house of the **Monitor.** Buchanan was peering through slit in the pilot house armor when an iron splinter struck him, and caused him to temporarily loose his sight. Since he was unable to see he was forced to withdraw from the fight.

In the confusion that follows another officer who was the Exec a Lt. Samuel Dana Greene took over command and returned to the battle.

The **Virginia,** whose Captain was under the impression that the Monitor had withdrawn, and since the **Minnesota** was somewhat out of reach decided to withdraw.

Damage to the **Virginia** required repairs and convinced that she had won the battle, the order to withdraw was given.

The **Monitor** arrived back on the scene to see the **Virginia** retiring and retired also.

Each Commander felt that he had won the day where it had been essentially a draw.

Later information revealed that although the Southern forces inflicted more damage, the coastal blockage was not broken.

Union ships tightened the blockage of the South and the **Virginia** was bottled up in Hampton Roads. Her presence did prevent Union ships from using the James River but that was the only long term benefit.

THE EFFECTS OF THE BATTLE BETWEEN THE MONITOR AND VIRGINIA

When word of the battle reached other countries around the world, a frenzy of ship building, like the **Monitor**, erupted in all countries that had a navy. The Union built river **monitors** for controlling the Mississippi river and cutting the Confederacy in half.

The Union immediately began constructing 10 more monitor type ships of bigger design. Although the monitors were effective on rivers, the rough waters of the ocean made them much less effective.

Russia also launched a **monitor** type ship building program.

England began installing rams on its warships. This concept became standard on warships up until the onset of World War I. The improvement of naval guns made close encounters almost suicidal.

This advance in Naval Warfare was another link in the chain of events that lead to the sinking of the Cruiser Helena in Kula gulf in 1943. The invention of the first iron clad vessels by the Confederacy and the Union revolutionized war ship building world wide.

EVENTS THAT INFLUENCED THE DESIGN OF CRUISERS

The Treaty signed as detailed below determined that the Cruiser **Helena** was built and the Specifications used in her construction, which left a lot to be desired.

During the First World War in France, England and Japan had formed an alliance. American interest viewed this alliance as a potential threat. As a result American naval planners began drawing up plans to build a two ocean navy. The intent was to build a navy that would be as powerful as the combined navies of England and Japan. Conversely England and Japan perceived such a large navy by the United States as a threat to their interests. All governments realized that such large expenditures on building a large navy would cost a large amount of money. Great Britain's involvement in World War One had cost a great deal and as a result their economy was weak financially. As a result the three countries started to discuss a way of avoiding an Arms Race that would be acceptable to all three countries.

Therefore a Naval Arms Treaty was held in Washington DC in 1921. The intent of the Treaty was to limit the number and size of battleships, battle cruisers and aircraft carriers each country could build and man. These three types were considered to be expensive 'capital' ships. The terms of the Treaty would reduce the size of the various Fleets. It would only allow the construction of new ships to replace older ships being taken out of service. However there was one exception and this exception involved smaller ships such as cruisers. As a result all three countries then embarked on building larger cruisers to partially replace the need for battleships. This loop hole in the treaty led directly to the building of ships like the **Helena**.

The United States lead this type construction as the ships that were needed would be capable of cruising long distances at high speed with extended range in the great distances of the Pacific. A large hull was needed to accommodate the need for greater fuel storage and larger power plants allowed heavier armor and larger guns to be included in the design. A new category emerged in that Cruisers that were built were classified as "light" or "heavy" cruisers. Light cruisers mounted guns no larger than 6 inch. This restriction applied regardless of the size of the vessel. Ships with 8 inch guns or large were classified as "heavy" cruisers. Cruisers of the World War One era weighed in at 3,500 tons whereas the newer ships weighed in at 8,000 tons for light cruisers and 12,000 tons for heavy cruisers.

As a result in retaliation Britain and Japan began to build ships to match the American designs. A cruiser Arms Race started between the three countries. All three countries began to realize the cost of such an Arms Race and so another Treaty was signed in 1930 that was intended to limit the number of cruisers each country could build and the tonnage of each type. Under the terms of the new treaty the maximum size of a cruiser was set at 10000 tons and a further restriction was placed on the total tonnage of each fleet of cruisers. To arrive at a comparative evaluation of one battleship versus more than one cruiser, it was felt that one 45000 battleship was comparable to four 10000 ton heavy cruisers or ten 4500 ton light cruisers. **The new American designs covered a broad range from lightly armored 5000 ton ships that carried 12 inch guns while heavily armored 10000 ton ships carried only 6 inch guns.**

So it was because of these two Treaties that light cruisers like the Helena were built the way they were in the first place. She was under gunned and had inadequate armor.

RISE OF THE JAPANESE NAVY

Without such a powerful Navy Japan would never have been a threat to the United States. And without the Japanese Long Lance torpedo the **Helena** would not have been sunk in Kula Gulf in 1943.

Although the Japanese Islands number into the hundreds, with many bays and inlets, Japan lagged behind other Nations in building ships for the sea.

There were early invaders of Japan and the Japanese fought wars against their enemies. The pages of history reveal that in the 13th century a Mongol fleet came to Kiushiu. Japan did not have vessels capable of repelling the invaders. Later at the close of the 16th century Japanese armies were fighting Koreans. The Korean war-junks repeatedly defeated the Japanese Squadrons. This superiority decided the conflict on the land and the sea.

Great Galleons with high masts and clouded with sails had visited Japan from Portugal, Holland and England. Still the Japan did not attempt to emulate them. The visits by these ships occurred in the second half of the 16th century. *Two ships were built by an English Pilot* but an edict vetoing construction of sea-going vessels was issued in 1636. This edict was part of the Tokugawa policy of isolation.

American ships that visited Yedo bay in 1853, coupled with the urgent counsels of the Dutch that caused Japan to adopt a different policy as concerns building vessels for the sea.

In 1855 a training station was opened in Nagasaki. *A Dutch maritime person served as instructor.* A building-slip and an iron factory were established at Nagasaki. Shortly afterward a naval school was organized at Tsukiji. *The Dutch presented a war-ship, the Kwanko Maru, to the Shogun's government to be used in training cadets.*

Between 1857 and 1858 two more vessels were added. One came from the Dutch, and the second one was a present from Queen Victoria. These two vessels became the Nucleus of the new Japanese Navy.

For the first time, a Japanese ship crossed the Pacific in 1860. The ship was the Kwanrin Maru. *Later young Japanese officers were sent to Holland for instruction in naval science.*

France and the Dutch played a significant part in Japan's building a Navy but it was to the British that Japan turned for instruction in the art of maritime warfare. Little did these Englishmen realize that they were sowing the seeds that one day would obliterate them from Asia and strip them of all of their possession's. It was like an individual digging his Own grave.

After a bit of political turmoil the Japanese found themselves in possession of a squadron consisting of 17 warships that weighed in at 13,812 tons displacement. Two of these vessels were armored, while one was a composite ship. The others were all constructed of wood.

Recognizing the need, a naval college was built at Tsukiji. Instructors were requested from England. 30 officers and one warrant officer Commander Archibald Douglas headed the contingent.

Many other things occurred. The first steam war-ship constructed in Japan was a gun-boat of 138 tons and was launched in 1866. It was launched at a building-yard located at Ishijawajima. This location was near the mouth of the Sumida river; the present site of the city of Tokyo.

At the above yard and one at Yokosuka two vessels of 897 and 1450 tons were built. These two vessels were launched in 1875 and 1876. By this time the Japanese had acquired the expertise of building and repairing vessels of considerable size.

Orders placed in England in 1875 resulted three years later in the construction of the Fuso, Japan's first ironclad of 3,717 tons and the Kongo and Hiei. These two ships were built with steel frames and were sister-cruisers of 2,248 tons.

Japanese sailors became expert in all things nautical. In 1878 a Japanese ship flying the Japanese flag appeared in European waters. This ship was the cruiser Seiki of 1897 tons that was built in Japan and was completely manned and operated by Japanese crews.

In the year 1882 30 cruisers and 12 torpedo boats were built. Although the program was extended, not one battleship had been built.

Plans were made in 1890 to build two battleships, but politics entered into the decision.

In 1894 Japan went to war with China. The Japanese navy at the time consisted of 28 craft for a total of 57,600 tons and 24 torpedo-boats. Among them was an armored cruiser of 4300 tons. China on the other hand had two ironclads of 8000 tons each.

In spite of having an advantage, China suffered defeats off the Yalu and Wei-hai-wei. Japan being the victor took possession of 17 Chinese craft, including one battleship.

Additional battleships and cruisers were ordered in Europe and when the Russo-Japanese War started the Japanese fleet asserted its superiority in the surprise (sneak) attack at Port Arthur. This battle occurred on the 10th of August in 1904. This important victory took place at Tsushima.

By the end of 1908 Japan had four naval dock-yards located at Yokosuka, Kure, Sasebo and at Maizuru. Twenty two vessels were built at Yokosuka by 1876. Included was one battleship of 19,000 tons. There was also an armored cruiser of 14,000 tons. There were two other yards that had not yet been used to construct heavy vessels. There were also two private yards one at Misubishi at Nagasaki and at Kobe. Several cruisers, gunboats and torpedo boats had been built at these yards.

Up until 1909 Japan was not completely independent in obtaining steel or in part of the ship building but had to use outside sources. A facility at Kure manufactured steel, which was sufficient for all of its needs.

By the year 1910, there were five Admiralties-namely Yokosuka, Kure, Sasebo, Maizuru and Port Arthur. In addition there were four naval stations. These were located at Takesiki and Mekong, Ominato and Chinhai.

In 1910 the navy had conscripts and volunteers. About 5,500 were taken by 1910. This was approximately about 55 percent to 45 percent. The length of service was 4 years, followed by 7 years in the reserves. About 200 cadets were added each year. By 1906 there were Admirals of the Combat Class and non-combative in the amount of 77. Officers, combative and non combative ratings below the rank of Admiral totaled 2,867. In addition there were 9,075 Warrant officers. 29,667 were blue jackets. Cadet totaled 721. The overall total was 42,407. At the time the highest educational institute was the naval staff college. There were five classes for officers alone.

Junior engineers, warrant-officers and blue jackets attended gunnery and torpedo schools. There was also mechanical schooling for selected individuals. Meanwhile the Naval Academy was relocated from Tokyo to Etajima.

Officers attended the Academy for three years, and had an additional year at sea. Finally, there was a naval engineering college collateral to the naval academy. This completed their training.

From 1882 Japan had been able to perform their own instructions in naval warfare. From 1886 forward Japan had been able to manufacture her own prismatic powder. From 1891 she had been able fo manufacture her own quick firing guns and Schwartzhopf torpedoes. A very potent explosive titled Shimos powder, a very powerful explosive, was invented by a Japanese.

Over a span of 50 years Japan had advanced more in self sufficiency, in the construction of naval vessels and in having highly trained crews to man them than any other country. Japan was unified in 1868 and the Imperial Naval Fleet was established. Even though Japan could not equal the United State in Industrial Capacity she still had been able to assemble a military that defeated China and Russia.

Although those in the western military societies were not aware, Japans ambition was to be the most powerful nation in all Asia. Unfortunately Japan lacked raw materials and set out to correct that problem by conquest. It was also Japans desire to create a military that could challenge any other Military Force that might have designs on the far East.

By fighting China and Korea and later Russia Japan had large areas ceded to them. As part of the Japanese, Chinese treaty China ceded Korea and Formosa and paid a large indemnity.

The victory over the Russian Fleet allowed her to extend her boundaries by acquiring the Kuril Islands and parts of Manchuria.

As an Ally of the Western Powers against Germany she acquired the Marshall Islands, Carolina Islands and the Mariana Islands in the Pacific.

By the year 1920 Japan had the third largest fleet in the world. Although Japan was unable to equal the US in industrial capacity and had an economy only one-ninth that of the US she was still able to challenge the US in World War II.

In addition the Japanese Military Personnel involved itself in the Political Life of the country and strongly influenced its policies. By 1931 through political clout 32 percent of all moneys spent were devoted to the military. All of these maneuvers directly led in 1941 to the attack on Pearl Harbor.

In 1905 while engaged in warfare with the Russian; Japan acquired five submarines from the United States. After the war with Russia, Japan began manufacturing its own submarines. In addition seaplane carriers were built; mine warfare submarines and midget subs. By 1941 Japan had a fleet of 65 subs. At the time the US had only 23 subs.

Being a party to the Washington Naval Treaty in 1922 was one of the biggest mistakes the United States could have ever made. Under the terms of that treaty Japan was limited to 315,000 ton (on paper at least) but Japan had no intention of actually complying with the treaty limits.

The treaty allowed the United States a total of 525,000 tons and the US intended to comply with these limitations. To do so required the US to actually scuttle or scrap 15 battleships and cruisers that were partly under constructions. Japan on the their limit.

In the subsequent Treaty signed in 1930 Japan was limited to 108,000 for heavy cruisers; 100,450 tons for light cruisers and 52,700 tons for submarines. Japan had no intentions from the beginning of complying with either of the Treaty limitations. The Japanese Military schemed incessantly to achieve parity with the Americans. Since on paper Japan was relegated to a smaller Navy Japan then set out to achieve strategically what they were not able to accomplish in a material sense.

Operational and technological methods were explored to gain an advantage. In this vein long range torpedo combat tactics were developed. Also advanced night operation techniques were developed. Along these lines, powerful telescopes were built.

The overall approach was to be able to outrange the US Fleet under the sea, on the surface and in the air. Weapons to accomplish these goals were designed and built. Meanwhile the US was like a sleep walker, not realizing the danger that it was soon to be faced with.

In the early 1930's Japan developed the oxygen-propelled torpedo named the Long Lance. It not only traveled faster and farther than any torpedo used by the US or Great Britain, but it also carried a much bigger war head.

American warships Captains preferred approaching enemy naval vessels at less then 10 km (5.4 nautical miles) before opening fire.

Unfortunately the Long Lance Torpedo Type 93 had a range of 40 km (21.6 nautical miles or 24.9 land miles). Its warhead weighed in at 490 kilograms (1080 pounds) of high explosives.

The US torpedo by comparison range at a more modest distance and mounted a much smaller warhead.

Ironically for a Nation that has been the most inventive Nation in history had failed to grasp the principal feature of the torpedo. The range of a torpedo and the weight of the explosive charge it can deliver depends on only one thing. *That thing was the amount of Oxygen it has under pressure in its tanks. The US torpedo used compressed air which is only 17 percent oxygen. The Japanese Long Lance Type 93 used pure 100 percent oxygen giving it almost 6 times the range. Compressed air was used only to launch, then it switched to pure oxygen.*

What was even worse the US torpedo had a defective firing pin in the nose of it. So quite often even though it struck its target it failed to explode. The Long Lance almost never failed to explode. With it Japan almost wiped the US Navy off the map during the first 12 months of the Solomon campaign.

The many torpedo hits suffered by US Navy ships at such extreme ranges led US Navy officers to believe enemy submarines lurking near by in concert with the enemy's surface vessels were the culprits who were launching the torpedoes. In fact in some cases the Long Lance struck US vessels at ever longer range which misled the US officers to believe they had stumbled into a mine field.

In 1940 the Mitsubishi A6N "Zeke" airplane appeared in the Japanese Air Force. At the time it was the worlds best carrier based plane.

Fortunately for the United States and Britain, Japan did not have Radar at the beginning of World War II. However, in the field of optics and searchlight technology Japan knew no equal.

In the field of training of ships crews; technological innovation and tactical proficiency Japan was the equal of the US and Britain.

The world's first built-from-the-keel aircraft carrier was built by Japan. It was christened the Hosho. After its construction further design improvements were made. By 1941 this carrier and its complement of planes was a formidable weapon. The west had nothing to match it at the time.

Between the time between the end of World War I and the outbreak of World War II Japan and the United States had both focused on being ready to fight over the islands of the Pacific Ocean.

In 1940 Japan requested and received permission from France for Japan to land forces in French Indochina. (Why the French did this is a puzzle). Shortly after this acquisition the Prime Minister Dai Toa Kyoeiken declared the plan of a Great East Asian Co-Prosperity Sphere. Essentially Japan had the intent to figuratively rape all of the islands of their raw materials. But, that was not their announced goal; the stated goal was to benefit all of the island countries.

When Japan started landing troops in French Indochina the US reacted and placed an embargo on all steel and scrap iron being shipped to Japan.

Japan reacted and considered the American action as an

"unfriendly act". Japan demanded other Indochinese territory and when she started landing troops there the United States, Great Britain and the Netherlands froze all Japanese Assets in their possession. And all out embargo went into effect and a total embargo of oil was implemented.

The United States was almost Japans sole supplier of oil at the time. Without oil their fleet would shortly be unable to continue operating. The US naively felt Japan would concede and evacuate Indo China. It turned out to be something completely different.

In August of 1941 the Japanese military felt that war with the US was inevitable. They planned to launch a major assault on Asian targets. The main target at the time was the oil rich islands held *by* the Dutch in the East Indies and Malaya. Japan was sure this kind of action would lead to war with the US, therefore they also planned on invading the Philippines (at the time they were an American possession). Japan also planned to invade Guam, Hong Kong and Burma. The plot was that as soon as all of these targets were captured and secured a protective ring would be established around them. Japan felt at this point the US would sue for peace.

The Japanese Planners expected that it would take six months to consolidate their overall position of strength all over the Pacific, and this could be accomplished before the Americans could mount a counter-offensive.

To begin this planned offense an air attack was launched on Pearl Harbor on December 7, 1941, after Diplomatic Talks had broken down. The fact that the United States did not yield to Japanese demands was construed by Japan as a break down of the talks.

The Attack on Pearl Harbor will be mentioned late in the text of this novel.

The Gunboat Panay Incident in China

This incident indicated the long range plans by Japan to defeat the United States.

Japanese forces had occupied Manchuria in early 1937. At that time the United States had a small Asiatic Fleet that was intended to protect Embassy Personnel and any American tourist visiting China.

On December 12, 1937 the US gunboat **Panay** was attacked by warplanes from Japan. The attack was unprovoked and the gunboat was plainly flying the American flag. It was obvious that the Japanese had deliberately attacked. The gunboat was patrolling the Yangstze river when attacked. It was sunk in the attack and when surviving crew members tried to find concealment in the rushes in the shallows the attacking pilots strafed these survivors.

However, the higher up Japanese officials offered apologies and offered to pay retributions. The attack was obviously conducted by young hot heads who wanted to goad the United States into a war. Actually the higher ups offered phony apologies to gain time as the plans were already being prepared for a time of Japans own choosing.

The Japanese had invaded China in the summer of 1937 and moved in on the city of Nanking in December of the same year.

This **gunboat**, a flat bottom boat able to navigate the shallow waters, had evacuated the remaining Americans from the city on December 11 of 1937. Aboard at the time of the attack were five officers, fifty four enlisted men, four US Embassy staff members and ten civilians.

The attack had taken place the day after the evacuation. The **Panay** in company with three **Standard Oil Tankers** came under attack.

The **Panay** was hit by two of eighteen bombs dropped in the attack. The bombs were 60 kilograms weight equal to about 132 pounds. The bombs were dropped by three Yokosuka B4Y Type 96 bombers. It was also strafed by nine Nakajima A4N 95 fighters. In the sinking of the **Panay** three men were killed and forty three sailors and five civilians were wounded.

On the day after the attack on the 12th Japanese air forces had received word that Chinese forces trying to flee were aboard **ten large steamers** and a **large number of junks** (a unique type of Chinese **Rivercraft**) and at the time were reported to be 12 to 25 miles north of the attack site.

James C. Grew at the time was the American ambassador to Japan. He feared that the incident would provoke a war between the US and Japan. Grew remembered that the blowing up of the **American battleship** in Havana harbor in 1898 had triggered the war between the US and Spain.

The Japanese government had assumed full responsibility for the attack while still maintaining that the attacking pilots had not seen an American flag and assumed it was a Chinese craft.

It was reported that Japan paid out $2,214,007 in indemnity because of the attack.

However, US Navy cryptographers (those who spied electronically on all enemy radio transmissions) reported that they had intercepted radio messages between the enemy planes and their base. This intercepted messages clearly indicated that the attacking planes had been ordered to do so. This information was not revealed to any others outside the US military. The Individuals in charge of the US military knew only too well that the US was not up too a full scale war with Japan.

There was a great deal of controversy as to how to accept the rather large sum of money offered as indemnity. There was a lengthy and convoluted amount of controversy about the acceptance of monetary sums being paid concerning the sinking of the **Panay**.

The United States Navy Gunboat is the USS Panay. It plied the Yangtse river in China as a ship in the Asiatic Fleet.

INVENTION OF THE HEAVY THAN AIR FLYING MACHINE (THE AIRPLANE)

A main series of events preceded the Japanese Carrier Aircraft Attack at Pearl Harbor.

If Japan had not had the most powerful Air Force at that time they would not have been able to Sweep across the Pacific with such rapidity. Their 6 **Air Craft carriers** with their highly trained crews and Pilots could not be matched by any other Country at that time.

The convoluted series of events that led up to that fateful moment in time goes far back into the past. It seems that mankind has always dreamed of being able to fly like the birds. Even back in Leonardo De Vinci's time proposed vehicles were presented that would help men attain that goal.

Over a long period of time Hot Air Balloons and Gliders were constructed and tested, but the concept of manned flight eluded even the cleverest individuals.

SAMUEL PIERPONT LANGLEYS
EXPERIMENTS AND FLIGHTS

Many years of hard work had preceded his success. In fact on May 6, 1896 Samuel Pierpont Langley's Aerodrome No. 5 made the first successful sustained flight of an unpiloted, engine driven heavier-than- air craft of substantial size. It was launched from a spring-actuated catapult mounted on top of a houseboat on the Potomac River near Quantico, Virginia.

A Houseboat with a Ramp

Two successful launches were made on that day. Another flight was made on November 28, 1896. In that effort Aerodrome #6 flew for 4790 feet and was witnessed by Inventor Alexander Graham Bell.

After these successful flights using a government grant he built larger and larger craft and successfully tested them.

However, despite all of his efforts he was not able to achieve his goal of making the first manned flight of a heavier than air craft.

Langley had had a distinguished career in astronomy and shortly became Secretary of the Smithsonian Institute. He had also started a serious investigation into aerodynamics. This scientific work was performed at the University of Pittsburgh. Later in 1891 he published a paper titled "Experiments in Aerodynamics" which detailed the results of his experiments. After publishing this Paper he then devoted himself in building his designs.

Langleys Aerodrome Experimental Craft that crashed

A Photo of Orville Wright

THE FLIGHTS OF ORVILLE AND WILBUR WRIGHT

All of this changed one windy day on a beach located at Kitty Hawk, North Carolina.

The Records state that at about 10:30 in the morning of December 17, 1903 a man by the name of Orville Wright lay down on the wing of his experimental airplane. He and his brother Wilbur had constructed it after many months of experimenting and testing of model after model. They had even built wind tunnels to test many of their ideas.

But it was on that fateful morning with high consistent winds blowing from the north they decided to test their new plane on the sandy beach.

The engine which they had built was started. The engine and the propellers were run for a few minutes to get them in working order. The wind was gauged at 20 MPH. On slipping the rope the machine started increasing in speed to about 7 or 8 miles per hour. It lifted off from the truck just as it was entering the fourth rail. (The truck apparently served in place of today's landing gear). An onlooker standing by took pictures as the plane just left the tracks. His name was Daniels.

The flight lasted only 12 seconds and covered only 120 feet. That distance at present is less than the wingspan of some of the Passenger Planes of today. But, it was a momentous 120 feet.

It is also stated that three more successful flights were made the same day on that sandy beach.

It was Orville's brother Wilbur who piloted the plane on its second flight which was a record breaking flight. That flight lasted for 59 seconds and the distance that was flown was 852 feet.

They had begun their joint experiments in 1896 and that was 7 years before their historic flight. Their work was performed in their bicycle shop located in Dayton, Ohio.

The site of the test flights, prior to their manned flight, was selected because the beach at Kitty Hawk had almost constant winds that would aid their frail gliders in overcoming the pull of gravity. In all they made 700 successful unmanned flights.

When they were ready to test their first manned flight they were unable to find a manufacturer that could supply them with the required engine. No company could provide an engine that was both light enough and powerful enough to serve their purpose. So they designed and built their own engine.

In their excitement they notified several newspapers of their remarkable achievement but only one local journal covered the event in their paper. The newspaper reporters failed to realize the significance of this historic event that changed the World.

Photo of Scout Cruiser CL2 USS Birmingham With an Aircraft Ramp on her Bow.

The First Airplane Takeoff from a Carrier

The first plane to be launched from the deck of a US Navy ship occurred on November 14, 1910. The ship it was launched from was the Scout Cruiser SL -2 USS Birmingham.

Preceding this event in October 1910 a Captain W.I. Chambers traveled to Belmont Park, New York. At the time he was responsible for all aviation matters with the Navy Department. His mission for the trip was to inspect a new rather flimsy craft and to meet with pioneer aviators at the International Air Meet.

While discussing the possibility of using aircraft at sea he met Eugene Ely who was a pilot who worked for Glenn Curtis. Curtis was a builder of airplanes and had just built a Curtiss Pusher airplane. A pusher plane had the propeller mounted on the back of the plane with the propeller behind the pilot. This plane in a number of respects resembled the Wright Brother's plane flown at Kitty Hawk.

In a very short time financing was obtained and with the support of Assistant of the Navy Beekman Winthrop plans were made to attempt to launch the Pusher Plane off of a navy ship.

The ship chosen for this event was the Scout Cruiser Birmingham. A wooden ramp was constructed on the foredeck of the Cruiser at the Norfolk Navy Yard.

The ramp was designed by a Naval Constructor William McEntire. The ramp sloped down five degrees from the ships bridge to the tip of the bow. It was felt the pull of gravity due to the slope would help launch the plane on its 57 foot run down the ramp to the launch point.

The plane was loaded on board ship the morning of November 14,1910 and the engine was installed as the ship left port by Ely with the assistance of his mechanics.

The ship left port before noon and sailed down the Elizabeth River to

Hampton Roads where the launch was to take place. Unfortunately the weather was stormy with rain squalls. The ship anchored hoping to ride out the weather.

In mid-afternoon the weather subsided and the ship winched in the anchor. As the ship got underway Ely who was to pilot the plane warmed up the engine and checked out its controls. Noting that the weather was starting to get worse he decided to launch it.

At 3:16 pm he reved up the engine to full power and gave the release signal. The plane rolled down the ramp and became airborne.

The plane briefly touched the water and the spray damaged the propeller. This caused the plane to shake heavily and he was forced to land on a nearby spit of land. The spit was Willoughby Spit. He landed only five minutes after being launched and the flight only covered two and one half miles. The landing was an emergency as Ely could not swim and the Plane was made out of pipes and had zero floatation capability. It is listed in the Records that there was a Chase Destroyer in attendance but the chances of the crew of the destroyer rescuing him would have not been encouraging in case the plane sank.

On January 18, 1911 Ely landed and took off from the **Armored Cruiser Pennsylvania** in San Francisco Bay.

In any event Lieutenant Theodore G. Ellyson began flight training that would make him the US Navy's first aviator.

In the photo Eugene Ely, who was the pilot, stands in front of the Curtiss Pusher plane. It was mounted on a platform that had been installed on the bow of the armored cruiser #4 **USS Pennsylvania**.

He is shown just before taking off. Earlier in the day he had landed on the ship's deck. This was the first time a plane had landed on a US Navy Ship's deck.

The ship at the moment lay at anchor in San Francisco Bay.

This plane was equipped with emergency floats under the wings to give it buoyancy in case the plane was forced to land in the water. The pilot's flying attire included rubber inner tubes that were worn around his shoulders to serve as life preservers. This version of the plane was equipped with a tricycle landing gear. Hooks located under the undercarriage were intended to assist in stopping the plane when it landed on the platform on the ship.

So it was this long chain of related events that one day led up to the six Japanese Carrier pilots that bombed Pearl Harbor and put the United States battleships out of World War II.

Photo # NH 77588   Eugene Ely with his airplane, before taking off from USS Pennsylvania, 18 Jan. 1911

ILL WILL BETWEEN EAST AND WEST

The ill will, or almost downright hostility of Japan towards the United States, went all the way back to Admirals Perry's visit there in 1853.

His rude and brusque and ill manners did not go over very well with the Japanese. His insistence on intruding into their Holy City was taken as an affront.

The crude weapons that the Japanese had at that time must have emboldened him. His marching through the Japanese city with 300 of his marines, who were heavily armed, would not exactly endear him to any nation, not only the Japanese.

It was really uncalled for, for him to order his gunners to fire on some of the buildings, located near where his ships were anchored It was clearly a threat and was intended to intimidate the Japanese, if they did not accede to his demands.

The ill will engendered in that event could very likely linger even at this late date.

The reasons for an intense dislike of all things British by the Chinese would be understandable to most anyone.

British Merchants controlled the Opium Trade in China. The addiction of a huge number of Chinese was a source of vast income for the wealthy business men of England. These individuals were not going to give up this lucrative source of income no matter how immoral it surely was. To profit by the misery of other unfortunates is despicable regardless of who practices it.

The First Opium War between China and England started in 1839 and lasted until 1842. The Qing Dynasty attempted to restrict Britain's Opium Trade, but were unsuccessful.

A Second Opium War erupted in 1856 and lasted four long years until 1860.

At the time Opium was not prohibited in Great Britain or Ireland.

Opium was smuggled out of British India into China in defiance of Chinese Prohibition Laws.

William Gladstone, a prominent English Statesman was openly critical of the Opium trade that England was involved in.

China was defeated in both wars and was forced to sign two treaties. The treaties were the Treaty of Nanjing and the Treaty of Tianjin. In these treaties provisions for opening of additional ports to unrestricted foreign trade was provided. Also that there would be fixed tariffs. In addition China was forced to cede Hong Kong to Britain.

Several other European Countries adopted England's lead and demanded equal rights that were agreed too.

Many Chinese deeply resented the feeling of humiliation that the treaties engendered. These feelings of resentment led directly to the Taiping Rebellion that lasted from 1850 to 1864, a period of 14 years. The Boxer Rebellion followed in 1899 and lasted until 1901. In 1912 the Qing Dynasty fell and this brought an end to dynastic China.

The US Battleship USS Maine in Havana Harbor

THE SPANISH - AMERICAN WAR

This incident led to the United States acquisition of over seas colonies, some of which were in Asia. This acquisition of colonies further infuriated the Japanese as they resented any Western intrusion in their area of the world.

Up to the year 1898, Spain had the overseas colonies of Cuba, Puerto Rico, The Philippines, and Guam. Spain also had the colonies of Spanish West Africa, Spanish Guinea, Spanish Sahara, Spanish Morocco and the Canary Islands.

In 1898 a revolution was taking place in Cuba. A small armed uprising against Spanish authority was underway. In 1896 Captain General of Cuba, General Valeriano Weyler took action to suppress the insurgency. His plan was to isolate the rebels from their sources of supply. As part of this plan over a period of time he had more than 300,000 rebels confined in concentration camps. It was reported that conditions were so squalid that at least 100,000 people had died.

In the United States at the time there was a large number of Cuban émigrés. This group was very vocal in supporting the revolution and contributed large sums to support it. The news in the American press of the atrocities being practiced inflamed public opinion.

Things reached a point where the battleship USS **Maine** was dispatched to Havana. The Maine dropped anchor there on January 23, 1898.

Just prior to the arrival of the Maine riots had broken out and this prompted the US to land marines to protect American citizens in Havana. No harm had come to any Americans at that time.

Pro Spanish Cubans began to feel a growing resentment of the American support for the revolutionist.

Unfortunately at this point, on February 15, 1898 a massive explosion aboard ship caused the **battleship** to sink. The supposed cause of the sinking was that a mine had been used. After a thorough investigation the reasons for the sinking were very murky. There were those who felt the explosion was caused by spontaneous combustion of the coal that was stored on board. The **Maine** was a coal burning ship.

In response to the growing tension the US expanded its army from 28,183 to 250,000 men.

In the States the press inflamed the public by accusing the Cuban government, affiliated with Spain, of deliberately blowing up the **Maine**. The **battle cry which then arose of, "Remember the Maine. To Hell with Spain**", rang out.

On April 19th American troops were dispatched to Cuba to end the civil war there.

In Congress the Teller Amendment was passed to ensure that the US would not establish permanent control over Cuba following the cessation of hostilities with Spain. This amended resolution demanded that Spain withdraw and authorized the president to use military force as he thought necessary to help Cuba gain independence from Spain. This ultimatum was signed by President McKinley on April 20, 1898 and was forwarded to Spain.

Upon receipt of the Ultimatum Spain declared War on the United States on April 25th.

The War between the United States with Spain resulted in fighting not only in Cuba but in the Philippines as well.

For the scope of this book, it is only pertinent to state that Spain lost the War and ceded Cuba, Puerto Rico, Guam and the Philippines to the United States.

The anger that arose later was that people in Cuba and in the Philippines believed the United States Forces would be withdrawn after the War with Spain was over.

Much to their chagrin they found on the contrary that they had merely traded one Master for another. This aroused hostility in both Countries against the United States.

After the War had ended the US Congress in its great wisdom pulled what essentially was a 'double cross' on Cuba. A follow up Amendment, the Platt Amendment was passed. Under this Amendment Cuba was prohibited from signing treaties with any other nation. Also Cuba was prohibited from accruing a public debt. Imperialist Forces in the United States pushed to extend American Power by retaining the colonies wrested from Cuba into the American permanent Sphere of Influence.

THE GREAT WORLDWIDE DEPRESSION OF 1929

Another link in the Chain of Events that led one dark night to the sinking of the Helena was the onset of the so called Great Depression. Due to the severe crisis generated in the United States by the financial collapse resulted in reducing the Navies effectiveness on the high seas.

What led up to and caused the so called Great Depression that descended on the entire World's financial establishment in 1929?

This Depression started in the United States and spread all over the world. It began in the United States with the collapse of the Stock Market.

In the massive cut back in all things financial the reduction in military spending was one of the worst. While Japan began to build the world's greatest sea going navy, the western world did not do anything to prepare for a future conflict. The same was true of England and France. Hitler began to build a monstrous war machine with giant tanks, a massive bomber and fighter air force and to train millions of fanatical fighters for his war machine.

Meanwhile the Western World with all of its inventive skills did nothing to be comparative. It was still felt that two great oceans were its protection from any harm abroad. The powers that be were living in a dreamland. They had forgotten that with the advent of the airplane the rules had changed. The airplane in a sense had caused the Earth to shrink.

The Great Depression caused wide spread suffering world wide. It led to a loss of confidence in the financial market and institutions. Nations like Germany, Italy and Japan looked to a Strong Man who could find a solution to the grievous problems that they faced.

Volumes have been written about the causes of the Great Depression.

It was not only the worst but it was also the longest lasting financial catastrophe the world had ever seen.

Many Banks had invested the depositer's money in the Stock Market, and lost it all. The Bankers had this naïve notion that since everyone else was making money, why shouldn't the Banks share in the Bonanza. They guessed wrong. When a Run on the banks (Depositors lining up in front of the bank demanding a return of their money) started, there was not enough cash on hand to meet the demand. Many people lost almost everything.

The passing of protectionist tariff policies made things worse as other nation retaliated by raising their own tariffs. As a result trade between nations dried up.

The Hoover administration was replaced by the Roosevelt New Deal. This change led to a major intrusion into the average person's life.

The United States started to ship vast quantities of scrap iron to Japan. Certainly the members of Congress could see the danger in something like this, but the times were desperate. Foreign Trade looked attractive, in getting dollars from overseas.

Finally in 1940 the United States began to spend large sums of money on the military. The Draft was also instituted.

It was surmised that the new emphasis on the mania to get rich quick, enjoy each new fad and to explore new ideas was a driving force in the madness. Traditional values of rural life were being replaced with a jazz-age young society. This breakdown in society was largely triggered by World War I. Farm boys had been introduced to wild living in Paris. There was a popular song that came out just after the War. Titled, "How you gonna keep 'em down on the Farm, after they have seen Paree (Paris)."

The wealthy made big profits, while people not so affluent spent more than they could afford. Easy credit contributed to the eventual collapse of the financial system. Farmers were faced with lower prices for their crops and growing debts.

The countries of Europe struggled to pay war related debts. This caused other financial problems.

Stock prices had been bid up to prices far above their actual worth. When the bubble burst and the Stock Market crashed it brought down the Banking System with it.

Desperate measures were tried by the Roosevelt Administration although none of them seemed to work too well.

One constructive effort was an establishment of the CCC or the

Civilian Conservation Corp. Thousands of young men were inducted into the Corp. These men built roads, dams, bridges and did massive public works projects nation wide.

According to the Records the International Banking Firms made large loans to countries that could not pay them back. This led to instability even in that financial institution.

It was estimated that between the years 1929 to 1932 world trade diminished by more than one half. In desperation all kinds of seemingly irrational techniques were tried, none of which seemed to work very well. Crops were deliberately plowed under to raise prices of food stuffs, meanwhile many in the public were on the verge of starvation. Cattle were herded into pits and shot to raise meat prices another fiasco.

This writer lived through that traumatic experience and has the opinion that the biggest problem of all was that, "The Public lost faith in the banking system and would not trust any of its money to any bank." Instead millions of them hid what little money they got in their mattress or buried it in their backyard in a sealed glass bottle. This writer knew personally one man who hid his money in a hole he dug in his basement until he was an old man.

Millions of young healthy white males rode on the tops of boxcars in freight trains traveling from one town to another in a desperate search for work. Shanty towns sprang up where these homeless men tried to find shelter. These 'shelters' were made of castoff cardboard boxes or discarded wooden crates used to ship fruit and vegetables.

During World War I with all of Europe in the grasp of a tragic war of annihilation the farms in Europe could not feed the people. The task of providing food fell on the United States. In this massive effort land that should have never been plowed up, was plowed up anyway. The individuals who farmed prairie land that should have remained as prairie walked away when the demand for food diminished and prices fell. High winds blew away the top soil that no longer had any vegetation to protect it. This writer personally saw the skies brown with dust that had been carried by the winds down to the Gulf Coast. The Gulf Coast was hundreds of miles south of Oklahoma.

All of these tragic events merely underscored why this Country failed to start building up its armed forces, with all of the danger lurking on the horizon from Japan and Germany.

Farmers pulled their autos with horses during the Great Depression as they could not afford gasoline.

A Crowd gathered outside of the New York Stock Exchange after the Stock Market Crash in 1929.

A crowd gathered outside of the New York American Union Bank during a Run on the Bank early in the Great Depression. Depositer's were trying to get some of their money back before the Bank ran out of money.

A Poor mother and children during the Great Depression in Elm Grove, California, USA in 1936.

A FIERY AMERICAN PATRIOT LIKE
PATRICK HENRY

The failure of the Admirals in the United States Navy to heed the advice of Billy Mitchell virtually drove the nail in the coffin of the United States prior to the onset of the attack on Pearl Harbor.

The next link in the chain of events that led to the sinking of the Helena occurred on December 28, 1879. On that date a son was born to John L. Mitchell and his wife. John Mitchell was a wealthy Senator from Wisconsin. The birth occurred in Nice, France. John Mitchell and his family came from a Milwaukee Suburb of West Allis, Wisconsin. The parents named the new infant William Lendrum Mitchell. He became famous and was called "Billy" by just about everyone who knew him, except those in the military.

Familiarity is not tolerated in the military.

As a young man Billy Mitchell attended Columbian College of the George Washington University. While there he was a member of the Phi Kappa Psi Fraternity.

At age 18 he enlisted in the United States Army as a Private. This happened during the Spanish American War. His fathers influence gained him a Commission as a Commissioned Officer. Billy joined the Signal Corp of the Army. He became an instructor at the Army's Signal School at Fort Leavenworth, Kansas. At the School even then he began to predict that wars of the future would be decided by airplanes not by battleships battering each other on the high seas.

He was one of the first persons from a prominent family to witness the Wright Brothers plane fly. In 1908 as a young man he observed Orville Wright conduct a flying demonstration at Fort Myer, Virginia. That experience transformed him and this was a major factor in his emergence as a prophet of the future might of air power. Following his new found passion he took flight instructions at the Curtis Aviation School located at Newport News, Virginia.

A considerable time later in his military career he had military tours in the Philippines and in the Alaska Territory. After completing these Tours he was assigned to the Army General Staff. At the time of his assignment he was the youngest member at age 32. His interest remained a strong compelling influence on him and he was assigned to the Aeronautical Division of the US Signal Corp. This organization later became the Army Air Service.

At the age of 38 in 1916 he took additional flying lessons on a private basis. He was forbidden by the Army to do so because he was considered too old (flying was thought to be a young mans game a the time) and because he was too high-ranking for the Army to take a chance on him dying in an accident.

General Mitchell

On April 6, 1917 the United States declared war on Germany after several provocations. As fate would have it Mitchell as a lieutenant colonel was sent immediately to France on further assignment.

Upon arrival in France Mitchell collaborated extensively with British and French prominent Air leaders. He studied their strategies intensely. It wasn't long before he had gained enough experience to begin preparations for American air operations. Very quickly he gained a reputation for daring. He was viewed as flamboyant and worked tirelessly as a leader.

Not long after he was elevated in rank to Brigadier General and was placed in command of all American air combat units in France. In the Battle of Saint-Mihiel he planned and led nearly 1,500 British, French and Italian pilots in the offensive. This is considered the first coordinated air-ground offensive in history.

Back in the states he became one of the most recognized individual along with Eddie Rickenbacker. His decorations included the Distinguished Service Medal, the Distinguished Service Cross and a number of foreign decorations.

After World War I ended in Europe, Mitchell returned to the United States in 1919. Upon his return he was appointed as the deputy director of the Air Service. He was allowed to retain his one star Generals ranking.

It was thought by knowledgeable sources that he would be appointed as Director of Air Services. Instead one of his classmates, a General Charles T. Menoher was appointed instead by General of the Army Pershing. General Menoher had commanded the Rainbow Division of the US army in France in W W I.

General Mitchell's relations with his Superiors became more and more strained, as he continued to verbally, almost berate them for their shortsightedness concerning the emergence of Air Power as the dominant weapon of the future. His personal verbal attacks were against Highly Placed individuals in the military in the War and Navy Departments.

He repeatedly advocated the development of bombsights, ski-equipped aircraft for operation in the Artic Regions, superchargers on aircraft to make them faster and the development of aerial torpedoes. This particular weapon in the following World War II became a fearsome weapon.

To keep the subject constantly before the public he advocated using airplanes to fight forest fires, conduct border patrols, push for improvement in performance of aircraft in speed, endurance and altitude records.

According to the Records at that time his primary focus was on the tremendous costs of building battleships and battle cruisers. It was his relentless contention that, "A Force of anti-shipping airplanes could defend the coastline more economically than the installation of fixed Coastal Guns or Naval Vessels". He insisted that a thousand bombers could be built for the same cost as one battleship. The Naval Brass was infuriated when Mitchell stated publicly that he could sink any warship by bombs delivered from an airplane.

Specifically he boasted that he and his flyers could sink an enemy captured German battleship if only given the opportunity.

Earlier in response to Mitchell's claims the Navy had quietly conducted its own bombing attack on an old battleships, the Indiana, near Tangier Island, Virginia.

A Captain William D. Leahy released a statement meant to silence Mitchell. The statement read as follows: "The entire experiment (the navy bombing test) pointed to the improbability of a modern battleship being either destroyed or completely put out of action by aerial bombs."

To the embarrassment of the Navy Brass the New York Tribune revealed to the public that the so called Navy Bombing Tests had been rigged. The public was made privy to the fact that the battleship had been bombed with dummy bombs filled with sand. The actual sinking was a result of high explosives that had been placed aboard before the bombing and detonated remotely.

When Congress became aware of this chicanery two resolutions were passed urging that new tests be conducted. The Navy had no choice but to accept General Mitchell's challenge.

The Navy Big Wigs still had not accepted defeat but continued to try and rig the results. This was done to prevent any open accounting of what actually took place. To accomplish this nefarious scheming the Navy insisted that a news blackout would be imposed until the results had been analyzed (sanitized).

As another attempt to thwart any honest testing, at this critical moment, the Chief of the Air Corps tried to have General Mitchell dismissed from the Service a week before the said Tests were to be conducted.

A Comment by the Author: Any man who has ever served in the Regular United States Navy learned early on that one of the Cardinal Rules is that, "A Junior member of the military never, never, never challenges a Senior Officer, even if the Senior Officers actions are questionable." From this Author's actual experience in a Combat Destroyer Squadron, this refusal to face facts by these high ranking Navy Officers, almost caused the US to lose the War with Japan in 1942 and 1943.

The 1st Provisional Air Brigade with its supporting air and ground crew of 125 aircraft and 1,000 men was assembled at Langley, Virginia. This took place on May 1. 1921. Six squadrons from the Air Service participated.

General Mitchell took personal command on May 27th after bombs, fuses and other equipment had been tested. The tests were conducted at the Aberdeen Proving Grounds. After completion of the tests training was begun in anti-ship bombing techniques.

A veteran Russian pilot who had bombed German ships in World War I participated in the training period. His name was Alexander Seversky. It was his suggestion to General Mitchell that his flyers should try to land their bombs alongside the target ship instead of hitting it directly. It was felt the explosion in the water adjacent to the ship would cause the side of the ship to cave in. It would be like later explosions from a torpedo striking a ship below the waterline.

General Mitchell conferred with a Captain Alfred Wilkinson Johnson who was a Commander in the Air Force in the Atlantic fleet. He was assigned to the USS Shawmut. He confirmed that near miss bombs would indeed inflict more damage than damage from direct hits would.

In effect the explosion would drive a massive amount of water away from the ship, when it came crashing back it would cause the face plates to fail leaving a gaping hole in the side of the ship.

In spite of the restrictions placed on General Mitchell's flyers several ships were bombed and sunk. On June 21, July 13 and July 18 an ex-German destroyer G102 was sunk. An ex-German light cruiser Frankfurt was also sunk.

A 2,000 pound bomb near-miss damaged the Ostfriesland's stern plates. This German battleship was considered unsinkable. It took a number or bombs to finally sink the above ship. The attacks were compounded by interference from high ranking Navy officials.

The 'Unsinkable' German battle ship Ostfriesland's

Conflicting opinions were expressed over the success of the bombings by General Mitchell and the Navy Brass.

The final result was that General of the Army John J. "blackjack" Pershing hoping to smooth the Navies ruffled feathers downplayed the results of the bombing to the public.

There was one positive thing that came from the tests in that budgets were revised for further air developments and forced the Battleship Admirals reluctantly to consider the possibilities of Naval Airpower.

Subsequent bombings from the air sank the pre-dreadnaught **Alabama** in 1921. The battleships **Virginia** and **New Jersey** were sunk in 1923.

In 1922 General Mitchell met Giulio Douhet who was an Italian aviator who shared his views as to the power of military aircraft. Mitchell translated Douhet's "The Command of the Air" into English.

In an attempt to silence Mitchell he was ordered to Hawaii and then to Asia. The attempt backfired as upon his return General Mitchell promptly published a 324 page report on his predicted future war with Japan. Included was his contention that an attack on Pearl Harbor was a strong possibility.

General Mitchell was correct in his assessment of the utilization of carrier aircraft in such an attack. His book was titled **Winged Defense**.

He was quoted as saying at the time, "Those interested in the future of the country, not only from the national defense standpoint but from a civil, commercial and economic one as well, should study this matter carefully, because air power has not only come to stay but is, and will be, a dominating factor in the world's development."

General Mitchell remained at odds with several very powerful individuals in the military. Among these were Major General Charles T. Menoher and Mason Patrick. These two men were his immediate Superiors at the Lampert Committee hearings in front of the US House of Representatives. Mitchell severely castigated the Army and the Navy's Leadership at these hearings.

After his testimony before the House of Congress General Mitchell was reduced in rank back to his permanent rank of Colonel. This demotion was followed by his being transferred to San Antonio, Texas as an air officer to a ground forces corps. This was seen as punishment and exile for his recalcitrant manner. His transfer had been at the behest of the Secretary of War John Weeks.

At this tense juncture the Navy dirigible Shenandoah crashed in a storm. 14 of the crafts crew were killed and three seaplanes were lost on the flight from the West Coast to Hawaii. After this happened Colonel Mitchell issued a public statement accusing several senior leaders in the Army and Navy of incompetence. He added the statement that, "Their actions were almost a treasonable administration of the national defense."

Apparently the Navy Brass could not condone this direct public affront any longer. In November of 1925 he was court-martialed at the direct order of President Calvin Coolidge. A Frank Reid served as Mitchell's chief counsel.

A Scene at the Court Martial of General Mitchell

It was reported the trial itself drew great public attention and support. However, the military tribunal found Colonel Mitchell guilty of insubordination, and suspended him from active duty for five years without pay.

The generals acting as judges wrote that, "The Court is thus lenient because of the military record of the Accused during the World War."

The case had been presided over by Major General Robert Lee Howze.

Mitchell resigned instead on February 1, 1926. He spent the next ten years writing and preaching air power to anyone who would listen.

Mitchell believed that President Roosevelt was a strong Navy Advocate. It is reported that for a time he had hopes of being appointed as assistant secretary of war or perhaps even as secretary of defense in a new and unified military organization. Neither prospects ever materialized.

Mitchell died of a variety of physical ailments which included a bad heart and a massive and extreme case of influenza in a hospital in New York City on February 19, 1936.

An so **a fiery Patriot in the mold of Patrick Henry left the scene, but his predictions proved to be true in the Attack on Pearl Harbor and in the Solomon's Campaign in the Far Pacific in 1942-43.**

Incidentally one thing of great importance took place during the bombing attacks by General Mitchell's flyers. At these bombing exercises were a number of Observers from Japan. After witnessing these bombing attacks the Japanese took General Mitchell's admonitions to heart and started building the greatest Carrier Air force the World had ever seen.

And that Carrier Air Force almost swept the United States Navy from the Seas, but for the Grace of God.

But the obstinate reactionaries in the US militaries refusal to face facts had long term adverse consequences.

A World Caught Up In Flames

Another link in the Chain of Events occurred on April 20, 1889. On this date an infant boy was born in the Gasthof zum Pommer at an inn in Braunau am Inn located in Austria-Hungary. This Inn was located in Bavaria. Bavaria is located in the southern part of Germany where it fronts on Switzerland and is in view of the Alps.

His father tried his hand at farming when he was quite small but the farming effort did not go well. During this period the boy seemed to have a happy, carefree childhood.

However as the years passed by he experienced many failures in the various ventures that were important to him. Although he had ambitions to be an artist, he was a failure. His father was a tradition-minded authoritarian individual who frequently beat him.

He rebelled when forced into vocations that were against his will. Over the years the Surrender Terms at the end of World War I began to arouse a great deal of resentment in him.

When World War I broke out he served in the 16th Bavarian Reserves in the army and saw action in France and Belgium. His rank was as a Gefreiter (private first class). He served as a runner delivering messages on foot on the battlefield. This was a very dangerous assignment.

He participated in a number of major battles on the Western Front. Among these battles were the First Battle of Ypres, Battle of the Somme, Battle of the Arras and the Battle of Paachendaele.

A Photo of Adolph Hitler as a soldier during the First World War (1914-1918)

In one of these battles 40,000 German soldiers were killed. His Company of 250 in the 20 day battle was reduced to only 42 that were not killed or wounded.

He was decorated twice for bravery. Among his awards were the Iron Cross Second Class in 1914 and the Iron Cross First Class in 1918.

He was wounded and spent time in a military hospital but returned to the Front after recuperating. On October 15, 1918 he was temporarily blinded in a mustard gas attack, but recovered his sight.

Over the years he had become a passionate German patriot although he did not become a German citizen until 1932.

A comment: "He was an evil man, but not a coward on the battlefield."

Front, left is Herman Goring who was Hitler's Chief of the German Air force (Luftwaffe).

THE MAN WAS ADOLPH HITLER

Over many years he affiliated himself with radical and very brutal men and on July 29th, 1921 Hitler became the Fuhrer of the National Socialist German Workers Party.

His great moment came with the onset of the World Wide Great Depression. He became the Reichskanzler (Chancellor) of Germany on January 30, 1933. He committed suicide in his Bunker in Berlin on April 30, 1945.

His death camps caused the deaths of millions of unfortunates.

Between those two years his Panzers, Air Force and Navy almost wiped Civilization as the Western World knows it, off the map.

At a time when it seemed that Britain would fall to the might of the German Military, the Japanese came to the conclusion that this was the time to strike.

The Attack on Pearl Harbor was launched and the United States entered World War II.

Below is a a Photo of the Signing of the Treaty of Versailles that ended World War I.

EVENTS THAT PRECEDED
WORLD WAR II

After the surrender of Germany in 1918, Germany, Britain, France and the United States signed the Treaty of Versailles.

In accordance with the terms of the Treaty Germany was required to pay reparations; lost its overseas colonies; had their military severely weakened and with severe restrictions on that which remained.

The average German blamed the financial problems that arose on the terms of this Treaty. These resentments and the political instability led directly to the take over of the Government by Adolph Hitler and his National Socialist Party. As Chancellor he had absolute power over every German citizen as well as the military forces and the secret police.

In 1923 Benito Mussolini became Prime Minister of Italy. After his March on Rome Italy became a fascist state which overthrew the previous government. Italy became a totalitarian state with severe repression of all citizens. Mussolini had dreams of Italy once again regaining the pomp and glory of ancient Rome. He planned on doing this by conquering several of his weaker neighboring countries in the military sense.

Below is a Photo of Benito Mussolini (left) riding with Adolph Hitler (right) at the height of their power.

When Hitler came to power he withdrew Germany from the League on Nations. After taking this action he then formed a Rome-Berlin axis and signed the Pact of Steel. After the outbreak of World War II when the US joined the fray Japan also became an ally of Germany. Japan and Germany also signed the Anti-Comintern which was aimed at repelling Soviet Bolshevism.

Germany under the Nazis and the Soviet Union were mortal enemies. However, the signing of the Munich Agreement resulted in Germany's invasion of Czechoslovakia. This pact was followed by the signing of the Molotov-Ribbentrop Pact. Under the secret terms of this Agreement the two countries agreed to invade and partition Poland, the Baltic Republics and Finland between them.

Full scale war broke out in Europe on September 1, 1939. On this date Hitler's Panzers invaded Poland. This tragic event preceded the Attack on Pearl Harbor by 2 years 3 months and 6 days. During most of this period of time Britain faced the Nazi onslaught almost alone.

Three days after this act of war Britain and France declared War on Germany.

On the 17th of the same month Russia invaded Poland on the east. The Polish Government fled to Rumania and became a government in exile. This government in exile continued the struggle against the Nazi regime and had the world's largest resistance network.

After the fall of Poland there was a lull in the War until May 10th, 1940. Several other European countries were drawn into the conflict. Three Baltic countries permitted Russian troops to establish bases and allowed troops in their territory. These Baltic Republics were occupied by the Soviets in June of 1940 and were annexed in August of 1940.

The Soviets tried to annex Finland and offered to sign a Union Agreement. When Finland refused, fighting broke out between Finland and Russia. After three months of heavy winter fighting, and having suffered heavy losses, the Soviet Union withdrew. However, the Finns had to sign the Moscow Peace Treaty. As a Condition of the Treaty, Finland had to cede 10 percent of its territory to Russia.

On May 10, 1940 Germany launched an attack on Belgium, the Netherlands, Luxembourg and France. After by- passing the French fortifications known as the Maginot Line (by going around the unfinished northern end) German army units swung its Panzers against the French. The German attack was through the Forest of the Ardennes. The French had erroneously assumed that this forest could not be penetrated by any enemy army.

The fighting between France and Germany only lasted for six weeks and the French surrendered on June 22, 1940. Many French soldiers managed to escape to England.

The Soviets had a hand in the defeat of the French and British armies not realizing that in the near future the full fury of the German War Machine would be turned against them.

The retreating French and British forces were progressively driven back until their backs were to the sea at a place on the coast named Dunkirk. By almost a miracle, most of the British and a large contingent of the French were able to flee by sea to England. However, the English and French who managed to escape, unfortunately lost all of their military equipment.

A Nightime Scene at the Evacuation of the English and French Armys at Dunkirk

The Evacuation by Sea from Dunkirk

The Evacuation at Dunkirk lasted from May 26th to June 4th in 1940. The British and French forces had been driven to the beach at Dunkirk where they had their backs to the sea. A British and French rear guard tried to hold back the German military Forces trying to protect the Evacuation. Among the troops were also Canadians.

On the first day of the Evacuation only 7,010 were able to leave the beaches bound for England. Over this nine day period 850 vessels of all kind made the voyage from England to the beaches at Dunkirk. It was a motley group of vessels that participated from destroyers, ferry boats, yachts and various other types of sea going vessels. In addition were 42 British destroyers, helped along with 700 merchant boats, fishing boats, pleasure craft, and even lifeboats. This small fleet consisted of just about anything that would float. If not actually carrying the evacuees back to England at least they assisted in ferrying troop out to other vessels waiting off shore.

Over this period of time a total of 338,226 soldiers were evacuated. This group consisted of 198,229 British and 139,997 French troops.

It was a first believed that only a maximum of 45,000 troops would be evacuated, which would have placed England in great peril of being invaded by the Germans.

Naval Guns from the destroyers shelled the Germans and helped hold them back from the evacuation area.

Also the Royal Air Force outfought the German Air Force in the skies above the beaches. In this struggle in the air the RAF lost 474 planes while the German Air Force lost 132 planes.

The rescue of the bulk of the British, Canadian and a large contingent ensured that England would not seek peace terms with Germany.

A Photo of the only surviving British Spitfire Fighter that took Part in the Battle of Britain in the Air War.

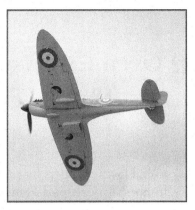

THE BLITZ OVER ENGLAND BY THE LUFTWAFFE

After England rebuffed several German offers for peace, Germany began to amass their air force in northern occupied France across the English Channel.

A Group of German Heinkel Bombers that were typical of those that participated in the Blitz.

The Germans began to make preparations for an invasion of England across the channel. Landing craft had been constructed and were beginning to be gathered prior to the attempt to gain air superiority in the Air over England.

This bombing attack on British cities by the Luftwaffe became known as the Battle of Britain. In the beginning the Luftwaffe concentrated on destroying the R.A.F. on the ground and in the air. Later the attacks were changed into bombing major and industrial British cities.

One significant event led to the eventual withdrawal of the Luftwaffe was, that a British pilot who got shot down and was still able to fly, just got into another plane and went back up. A German pilot on the other hand, who got shot down and survived, became a Prisoner of War. Besides the attrition rate on bombers became too great for the attacks to continue.

Hitler finally realized that air superiority could not be achieved and ordered a cessation of the bombing in September 1940.

In the bombing Britain's major industrial plants, cathedrals and civilians were heavily bombed. British citizens spent many a night in the Railroad Underground Tunnels (The Tube).

Among the cities most heavily hit were Birmingham and Coventry. Also attacks were launched on the naval base at Plymouth and the port of Kingston upon Hull.

At the time there were not any land forces in combat in the Europe Theater, but the war at sea continued. The Battle of the Atlantic between the German Submarine Wolf Packs and the British surface ships continued.

England launched a number of probing Commando raids on targets in Occupied Europe. In one such raid Commandos killed a number of high ranking German generals in a meeting near the coast. The Commando raid on Dieppe by Canadian Commandos ended in a disastrous defeat.

The British Spitfire was the plane the British used the most to fight the War in the Air.

The Air War began when British bombers began to make night time bombing raids on German targets. The British began these raids in 1939. The American Air Force entered the air war over occupied Europe and Germany from July 4, 1942 until the D-day invasion on June 5, 1944. From that point on the Air Force was used primarily in supporting ground operations.

The prewar planners expected that bombing of cities would cause the people to panic and that a rapid collapse would result. This turned out to not be as true as expected, at least by the German High Command.

One advantage the British and Americans had was that each had developed a large strategic bomber force. Germany on the other hand had concentrated on creating an Air Force that was used in conjunction with their ground forces. As a result the bombers that Germany built were smaller than their British and American counterparts. Germany never did build any bombers like the B-17 or the B-24 or the British Lancaster.

German bombing raids continued from September 7, 1940 until May 10, 1941. After that the German Air Force was involved in fighting against the Russians after the German invasion of Russia.

A Cut Away View of a German Buzz Bomb that was used to bomb England in the Air War between the RAF and the Luftwaffe (German Air Force Bombers)

Later German air raids continued on a smaller scale and were somewhat replaced by the Buzz Bombs (V1 Flying Bombs) and the terrifying V-2. The V-2 was a precursor to the eventual Intercontinental missile.

The attacks using the Flying Bombs and the V-2 diminished as England gained in strength and could attack the German Launching sites. However, in some locations the Germans had built underground, heavily constructed pens and in some case mobile bomb launching equipment. These attacks finally ceased when the Allied Forces overran the launching sites after the D-day landings and the subsequent military actions.

By the year 1942 the British and American Air Forces were able to launch at least 1,000 bombers in a raid. The British bombed by night, while the Americans bombed by day.

To illustrate the devastation wreaked in these raids, the German city of Dresden was obliterated in a fire bombing attack. It was estimated that between 25,000 and 35,000 people perished in this attack.

The point of this whole section of the novel is that, "If England had been successfully invaded by Germany, and if the Bulk of the British Army had not be rescued off the beaches at Dunkirk, World War II would have gone a completely different route and maybe even the Solomon's Campaign might never have taken place.

Another factor that led to the inability of the Luftwaffe to gain control over the skies of England was that the use of Radar helped the British to meet the attacking forces in the best manner. Also there was a large increase in the available searchlights for night firing.

The War in the Mediterranean and Balkans

The importance of this Campaign was that to an extent it occupied German Forces and led to a delay in the German Attacks that followed.

On April 7, 1939 Italy invaded Albania, a close by neighbor. Officially Italy had annexed Albania. The Italian Dictator Mussolini declared war on England and France on June 10, 1940. On October 28 Italy invaded Greece. The Italians had limited success in the War on Greece.

A Photo of the Harbor of Taranto during the 1930's.

On June 12 the Italians began a siege of the Island of Malta located in the Mediterranean. When the Italian Naval Forces Regia Marina met the Royal Navy and the Royal Australian Navy in fighting at sea in 1940 the Italians suffered a humiliating defeat. The Vichy French Navy suffered the same fate. The actions at sea were the attack on Mers-el-Kebir and the Battle of Taranto on November 11, 1940.

The Italians not only failed to defeat the Greeks but the Greeks were able to attack the Italians in Albania.

At this point the Germans intruded in the conflict. They were supported by forces from Hungary, Bulgaria. These forces invaded Yugoslavia. British, Australian and New Zealand forces were sent to intervene but were forced to withdraw. These Allied forces withdrew to the Island of Crete.

After capturing the Capital of Greece at Athens on April 27, 1941 the Germans then invaded Crete. This assault was carried out by large airborne troops. These paratroopers suffered great loss and were not able to prevail at once but later were able to do so. Most of the Allied forces on Crete were evacuated to Egypt on June 1, 1941.

Russo-German War
on the Eastern Front

Once the Germans had conquered the Greeks and driven the Allied forces out, Hitler prepared to launch his biggest attack, which was on Russia. However, the delay in defeating these forces delayed the Germans and this came back to haunt them on the Russian Front later.

It was on June 22, 1941 that Germany launched the invasion against the Soviet Union. The name given to this Operation was Barbarosa. It was the biggest invasion in history and also the bloodiest.

Over 30 million people were said to have died in it. It involved more combat units than all of the others combined. There was a total disregard for human life on both sides. It was a struggle to the death.

Ironically Stalin, the Russian Leader, was not prepared for the Invasion, although he had been warned repeatedly by the British that an attack was coming.

The early days of the invasion of Russia were a disaster. The Germans literally drove the Russians before them in a pell-mell retreat. Enormous numbers of Russian troops were captured.

According to the Experts that study history the German Campaign suffered from several flaws from the beginning. The most dominant factor was the vast nature of Russian Territory. The Germans had a daunting task of trying to keep there troops supplied with supplies because of the rapid advance.

The German advance came to a halt at the gates of Moscow for several reasons. The winter was setting in and their Army had outrun its supply train. The Germans came to a halt on December 5, 1941. The German Time Table had expected that Russia would have collapsed before this time.

It became apparent that if Hitler had not delayed by diverting forces into Greece earlier, and had not concentrated the Panzers on the Rumanian Oil Fields, perhaps Moscow could have been reduced.

One thing that compounded the Germans situation was that as the Soviets had retreated they had practiced a Scorched Earth Policy. All crops were burned, as well as all buildings. Wells were poisoned. Animals were shot if not used for food. The forests were burned as well as the grasses in the fields. The Germans advanced into a burned out wilderness.

During this paralyzing winter Soviet forces, mounted on ponies conditioned for the Artic like conditions, fell upon German supply trains, being pulled by horses, and slaughtered the Germans.

When spring arrived the Germans were systematically bled by the street fighting in the Russian cities. Finally Russian forces counter attacked and encircled the German Sixth army and forced the German general Von Paulus, to surrender. From then on it was a continuous German Retreat.

The vast tank battle at **Kursk** was probably the Germans swan song (The turning point of the entire War).

The basic point is that the Russians destroyed the flower of the German Army in front of Leningrad, Stalingrad and Moscow. If the American, British and Canadians had been faced with these forces in the Invasion on D-Day it is most likely they would not have prevailed.

It is stated somewhere in the Records, that towards the last stages of the struggle Germany was drafting veterans from World War I and even cadets (boys) from Military Academies.

THE JAPANESE ATTACK
AT PEARL HARBOR

On December 7, 1941 on a Sunday morning Japanese Naval Aircraft attacked US navy ships in Pearl Harbor. The attack was made without warning or after a formal declaration of war. At the time Peace Talks were being held in Washington D.C. between diplomats from both countries.

The purpose of the attack was to put the American battleships out of action so that they could not interfere with Japanese Operations in the far Pacific. These actions involved the British and Dutch naval and land forces.

In Pearl Harbor in the Attack were 8 of the 12 US battleships. The battleships **Idaho, New Mexico** and **Mississippi** were on duty in the Atlantic at the time of the Pearl Harbor attack. The battleship **Colorado** was in the Puget Sound Navy Yard located in Puget Sound Washington.

In the attack included were four US battleships sunk. Two were raised and returned to service. Four other battleships were damaged from bombs and torpedoes. Three cruisers, three destroyers and one minelayer were also sunk. 188 aircraft were destroyed mostly on the ground. Personnel losses amounted to 2,402 killed and 1,282 wounded.

The View the Japanese Pilots saw as they descended to attack ships of the United States Navy at Pearl Harbor.

Below is a photo of the battleship USS West Virginia during the Pearl Harbor attack. It was probably the most heavily damaged battleship that was repaired and put back in service.

Note: This Writer was a member of the crew on this ship from 1938 to September 1940.

A Photo of the USS Arizona. An enemy bomb hit a powder magazine and totally destroyed the ship.

Fortunately (for the US at least) the power station, shipyard, maintenance and fuel depot, torpedo storage facilities were not damaged. Submarine piers and headquarter buildings were also not damaged. This turned out to be a distinct disadvantage to the Japanese.

Japanese losses were minimal. Only 29 aircraft were destroyed. Four midget submarines were also sunk. Only 65 enemy personnel were killed or wounded.

This unprovoked attack caused the American Public that had been Isolationist before the attack, into a vengeful body thirsting for revenge. The battle cry rang out throughout the land, "Remember Pearl Harbor."

Germany promptly declared war on the United States. This caused the US to declare war on Germany and Italy and so the United States became involved in World War II.

The many causes that lead up to this tragic event were many and would be best obtained in other written accounts elsewhere.

A Photo of the Light Cruiser Helena during the attack on Pearl Harbor, The Helena is in the middle of the photo. She was torpedoed on the Starboard (right side) but did not sink.

The Cruiser Helena (CL-50) at Pearl Harbor

The **Helena** was commissioned at the New York Navy Yard on September 18, 1939. She weighed in at 10,000 tons. **Helena** saw service in the Atlantic in 1939-40 and after that she was transferred to the Pacific Theatre.

While tied up to dock #1010 in Pearl Harbor she was hit by a single torpedo during the Japanese air raid. Damage from the torpedo caused flooding in an engine room and boiler room. Repairs were made at Pearl Harbor and subsequently at the Mare Island Navy Yard located in Vallejo, California through June, 1942.

From the Records on the early morning of December 7, 1941 one of the crew on the **Helena o**bserved planes over Ford Island at about 07:57 am. The crew man who observed the planes had, had duty in the US Asiatic Station and promptly recognized them as Japanese. The planes when first spotted were at about 4,000 feet altitude. The Officer of the deck and Ensign W.W. Jones took immediate action. The member of the crew was a C.A. Flood, who was a Signal Man first class. The general alarm was immediately turned on which alerted all crew men aboard ship of the sighting of the planes. Simultaneously, over the general announcing system the words, "Japanese planes bombing Ford Island, Man all battle stations and break out service ammunition" was made. At the time, Flood was standing by the "Prep" signal for the morning 08:00 (am) Colors when the flag was run up. **Helena** guns began firing at the attacking planes at 08:01 (am).

Ammunition expended in the firing consisted of 375 rounds of five inch; 3,000 rounds of 1.1" and 5,000 rounds of .50 calibre.

An enemy plane launched a torpedo, while low over Ford Island, at a range of about 500 yards. The torpedo was released at about one minute after general quarters had been sounded and about one and a half minutes after the first sighting of the enemy planes. Meanwhile, the members of the crew of the Helena were all running to their battle stations. It was at this critical time that many of the crew received flash burns from the explosion and the concussion of the torpedo. It hit with a violent explosion on the starboard side at approximately frame 75 about 18 feet below the water line.

Following the torpedo the ship received four near bomb misses and suffered a few fatal casualties and a number of injured. One strafing attack followed but inflicted little damage. The strafing occurred just before the torpedo was released. At that time the crew had not reached their battle stations top side which prevented what would have been multiple injuries.

Damage sustained caused a temporary loss of power to the guns but it was quickly restored. Fires that had ignited were quickly extinguished. Several member of the crew manning the guns topside suffered injuries with one fatality.

By chance the **Helena** occupied a spot that had previously been occupied by the battleship **Pennsylvania** and as such was a prime target. Alongside the **Helena** during the attack was the minesweeper **Oglala** CM-4. The **Oglala**, having a shallower draft, allowed the torpedo to pass under her and strike the **Helena.** Water tight integrity was promptly insured as all water tight doors and hatches had been immediately closed and dogged down on the **Helena.**

The **Oglala** was no so fortunate. The blast from the torpedo underneath her caused her to sink.

The below two Japanese Carriers were damaged in the Battle of the Coral Sea and had to return to Japan.

A Photo of the Shokaku

A Photo of the Zukaku

The below photos is of two of the four Japanese Carriers that were sunk at Midway.

A Photo of the Akagi

A Photo of the Kaga on the way to attack Pearl Harbor with Akagi in background

The below are the other two of the four carriers that were sunk at Midway.

Photo of the Soryu while under construction

A photo of the Hiryu

A Sequence of Events just after Pearl Harbor

Japan had large military forces positioned all over the Pacific Ocean before the Attack on Pearl Harbor. The High Ranking Officials in Japan had planned to attack all across the Pacific if their demands in Washington DC were not met.

The following military catastrophes lead directly to the United States air raids on Tokyo by General Doolittles Planes:

December 7, 1941 Japan attacked the US Fleet in Pearl Harbor; Invaded Wake Island; invaded Guam. Declared War and bombed Philippines invaded Siam, Malaya and Hong Kong.

December 8, 1941 The US declared war on Japan.

Japan takes Gilbert Islands.

December 9. 1941 China declared war on Japan

December 10, 1941 The British warships the **Prince of Wales** and the **Repulse** were sunk by Japanese Planes.

Japanese Military Forces landed on Luzon in the Philippines.

December 11, 1941 Japanese Forces landed in Burma.

December 16, 1941 Japanese Forces landed in Borneo.

December 22, 1941 Japanese Forces layed siege to Manila.

December 23. 1941 Japanese Forces invaded Wake Island.

December 23, 1941 General MacArthur's Forces withdrew to Bataan.

December 24, 1941 Japanese were victorious in the Naval Battle of Makassar Straits.

December 25, 1941 Hong Kong surrendered to Japan.

December 31, 1941 Japan occupied Manila.

January 11, 1942 Japan invaded Dutch Borneo, Timor, Celebes and Dutch East Indies.

January 24, 1941 American destroyers were unsuccessful in opposing an Invasion Convoy off Balikpapan, Borneo.

February 13, 1942 Japanese Forces invaded Dutch the Oil Port of Sumatra.

February 15, 1942 Japanese Forces broke through last line of defenses of Singapore (a big British Base)

February19, 1942 US Naval Forces were unsuccessful in opposing Japanese Forces off Bali. Battle of Badoeng Straits was fought.

February 19, 1942 Japanese Admiral Nagumo's carrier planes attacked and wrecked the city of Darwin located in northern Australia.

February 27, 1942 US Navy suffered a disastrous defeat off Java.

March 7, 1942 British Military Forces evacuated Rangoon. Invaded Salamaua and Lae in New Guinea.

March 9, 1942 Dutch Military Forces surrendered on Java.

March 13, 1942 Japanese Forces landed in the Solomon's.

March 18, 1942 General MacArthur departed Corregidor, with his Staff, on **PT boats**.

March 18, 1942 Japan invaded Adaman Island located in the Bay of Bengal.

April 3, 1942 Japan began the siege of Bataan and the Fort of Corregidor, the last US Stronghold.

April 5, 1942 Japan raided Ceylon, Indian Ocean.

April 9, 1942 US Forces on Bataan surrendered to Japan.

April 10, 1942 Bataan Death March began. 76,000 Allied prisoners are captured . 12,000 are American.

5,000 Americans die on the march.

April 18, 1942 American B-25 Bombers raided Tokyo and flew to China.

May 7-8, 1942 Battle of Coral Sea occurred.

May 8, 1942 Corregidor falls; Philippines surrendered.

May 20, 1942 Burma surrendered.

June 4-6 Battle of Midway Island was fought.

June 7, 1942 Japan took the Island of Attu in the Aleutians.

August 7, 1942 US Marines landed at Guadalcanal and Tulagi.

August 9, 1942 Battle of Savo Island occurred.

August 24, 1942 Battle of Eastern Solomon's occurred.

September 26 Japan landed in Milne Bay, New Guinea.

October 11, 1942 Battle of Cape Esperance occurred.

October 25, 1942 Battle of Santa Cruz was fought.

November 12-15, 1942 The Naval Battle of Guadalcanal occurred.

November 30, 1942 Battle of Tassafaronga was fought.

January 2, 1943 Buna was taken on N. coast of New Guinea by US.

February 9, 1943 Guadalcanal was declared secured. Japanese Forces evacuated the Island.

March 2-4, 1943 The Naval Battle of the Bismarch Sea occurred.

April 18, 1943 Admiral Yamamoto's plane was shot down over Bougainville by US P-38 fighters. He was killed.

May 11 to June 30 US retook Attu in Aleutians.

June 21. 1943 US Forces invaded New Georgia Island.

August 6, 1943 The Naval Battle of Vella Gulf transpired.

November 1, 1943 Marines landed at Empress Augusta Bay on Bougainville.

November 5, 1943 Carriers **Saratoga** and **Princeton** raided Rabaul.

December 26, 1943 The Battle of Cape Gloucester was fought.

The Battle for the Solomon Islands ended, but the War on land, sea, air and under the sea continued.

The Carrier USS Hornet on the Tokyo Raid.
B-25 at take-off.

THE DOOLITTLE RAID ON TOKYO

On April 20, 1942 16 B-25 US bombers bombed Japan. This was the first American attack on Japanese soil.

After all of the disastrous news of the events transpiring in the Pacific the American Public was in a despondent mood.

At this time President Franklin Roosevelt had a meeting with his Joint Chief of Staff. At the meeting he expressed his desire to have Japan bombed, to raise American morale. He wanted this accomplished as soon as possible.

There was a Navy Captain Francis Low, who was the Assistant Chief of Staff for Anti-submarine Warfare. This Captain had noticed that twin-engine bombers in the Air Force were able to take off in the distance of the flight deck of a Carrier. On the runway at the airport the outline of a carrier deck had been painted. The airfield was located at Norfolk, Virginia. He reported his findings to Admiral Ernest J. King.

Further consideration of such a raid on Tokyo revealed that any bomber used must have a range of 2,400 miles one way. The planes would each have to carry a 2,000 pound bomb.

Several existing Army Bombers were considered. The **B-26 Marauder**, **B-18 Bolo** and the **B-23 Dragon** were all considered and rejected for one reason or another. For example, the **B-26** takeoff characteristics were questionable, if taking off from a carrier. The **B-23's** wingspan was 50% greater than another plane the **B-25**.This extra wing width would reduce the number of planes that could be carried on a carrier flight deck and would also endanger the Carrier's Island which was located topside on the edge of the Flight Deck.

The **B-25** fulfilled all of the requirements the best and was extensively tested. It passed all tests.

The subject of where the bombers would try to land after the Raid was discussed. If the planes could land in Russia the total flight distance could be reduced by 600 miles. Negotiations with the Russians were unsuccessful. Permission to land there had been denied. The only alternate place was the nearest coast of China.

After the selection was made, two **B-25** bombers were loaded on the flight deck of the **Carrier Hornet** at Norfolk, Virginia. After putting to sea, apparently out of sight of any prying eyes, the planes were able to successfully take off. However, they were unable to land on the carrier and had to return and land back at Norfolk. This test flight was conducted on February 3, 1942.

The Raid was approved by the Top Brass and planes from the 17th **Bomb Group** (Medium bombers) were chosen to provide the 16 planes required. The crews to fly the planes were all volunteers, although the crews were not informed as to what their targets were located. That was kept secret.

The Bombing Group the selected planes were to come from was moved cross-country from Pendleton, Oregon to Lexington, South Carolina to an air base located there. On the 17 February, 1942 24 bombers were detached from their bombing group.

To lighten the planes for the long flight the following modifications were made:

The lower gun turrets were removed.

De-icers and anti-icers were installed.

Steel blast plates were mounted on the fuselage around each upper gun turret.

Each liaison radio set was also removed.

Three additional fuel tanks and support mounts were installed in each bomb bay, crawl way and lower turret area to increase fuel capacity from 646 gallons to 1,141 gallons.

Mock gun barrels made of wood were installed in each Tail Gunner Cone. The existing Tail Gun were removed.

The Norden bombsights were removed for two reasons. The bombing was to be conducted from very low altitude, and secondly the Airforce did not one to fall into enemy hands if a plane crashed on enemy soil

Two of the bombers had cameras mounted to provide pictures of the Raid.

Three weeks of intensive training in taking off of a simulated carrier deck, painted on the runway, was conducted for the 24 bomber crews. These tests were conducted at Eglin Field, Florida. Training was also conducted in low-lever flying, night flying and over water navigation. Two of the planes were removed from the programs as one crashed and a second did not function properly.

On March 25, 1942 all the remaining **22 B-25's** took off and flew to McClellan Field located in California. A total of 16 planes were then flown to the Naval Air Station Alameda, California on March 31, 1942. This Air Station was located on the east side of the harbor of San Francisco.

On April 1, 1942 the 16 modified bombers, with their five man crews, were loaded on the Carrier Hornet. According to other sources of information the loading of the planes and the departure of the Carrier was conducted in a heavy fog so anyone on the shore would not observe the departure.

Each plane carried four 500 pound bombs. Three of these bombs were high explosive and one was a bundle of incendiaries. The incendiaries were in long tubes that were wrapped so as to be carried in the bomb bay. These were to separate after being dropped to increase the possible damage to enemy targets. Each bomber was equipped with two 50- caliber machine guns in an upper turret and one 30 caliber mounted in the nose. All planes were clustered closely on the flight deck and tied down in the order of their expected launch order.

The **Hornet** and **Task Force 18** left the port of Alameda at 10:00 am on April 7, 1942. A few days later this Force rendezvoused with **Task Force 16** in mid-pacific just north of the Hawaii islands. The Commander of **Task Force 16** was Admiral Bill Halsey, Jr. In this Task Force was the carrier Enterprise. The planes of the Enterprise would protect the **Hornet** while she was enroute to Japan; as the Hornet's planes were stored in the hangar deck.

The combined force included two carriers, three heavy cruisers, one light cruiser, eight destroyers and two fleet oil tankers. This combined force proceeded in total radio silence and darken ship at night.

On the morning of April 18, 1942 as the Task Force neared its launching point it was sighted by the Japanese picket boat number 23. The Captain of the picket boat immediately sent a warning by radio back to Japan that unknown vessels had been spotted. The picket boat was sunk by gunfire from the cruiser **Nashville**.

In a brief conference between General Doolittle and Captain Marc Mitscher, who was Captain of the **Hornet**, a decision was made to launch all 16 bombers immediately. The launch by necessity was 170 miles further from the intended launch point. It was also 10 hours before the previously scheduled launch time.

The bombers were re-spotted and the engines were started up to allow them to warm up. None of the bomber pilots had ever taken off from a carrier at sea, but all were able to be airborne safely. Launch began at 08:20 (am) and the last launch was made at 09:19 (am).

According to the Records the flight proceeded southwest toward the southern coast of Japan and crossed the China Sea. It was expected that several airfields in China in Zhejiang would display homing beacons after the Tokyo bombing. The bombers that reached this destination were then to refuel and fly on to Chungking. One of the bombers instead, headed for and landed in Russia.

The planes were faced with several difficulties as night was approaching, the planes were running low on fuel and the weather was getting worse.

After bombing Japan, 15 of the planes reached China partly because a tail wind increased their ground speed by 25 knots for seven hours. However it became apparent that none of the planes would reach their planned destination and would either have to bail out over China or risk a crash landing there.

After a flight of 13 hours the coast of China was reached and all crewmen bailed out or their planes crash landed. The bomber crew that landed in Russia was interned but later escaped to Iran in 1943.

Doolittle and his plane crew parachuted into China. They received assistance from Chinese soldiers and civilians.

All of the 15 bombers were lost and 11 crewmen were either killed or captured. The entire crews of 13 of the 16 bombers were returned to the US or to Allied control. Little damage was achieved on Japan in the raid. However, it did contribute to Japan withdrawing a carrier group from the Indian Ocean to defend the homeland thus weakening the Enemies strength in that theater.

One unfortunate unexpected consequence from the Doolittle Raid was that Japan executed at least 250,000 Chinese civilians as retaliation for their aiding the American Flyers.

The most important thing accomplished indirectly from the Doolittle Raid was that it influenced the Japanese Military in the attempt to take Midway Island. The Battle of Midway became Japan's "Waterloo." (The turning point of the Pacific War).

Note: If the Doolittle Raid had not occurred then the Battle of Midway Island probably would not have occurred. In that case Japan would not have lost the 4 carriers and their 200 pilots.

In that case the Japan Landing on Guadalcanal would not have been necessary as Japan could have continued their offensive using the carrier aircraft as their primary offensive weapon. As a result the Battle of Kula Gulf would not have taken place and the Helena would not have been sunk. This was another link in the Chain of events.

A Photo taken of the carrier USS Lexington on fire at the Battle of the Coral Sea.

THE NAVAL BATTLE OF THE CORAL SEA

In early 1942 Japanese Military Forces had conquered nearly all of Southeast Asia. The new British battleships, **Prince of Wales** and **Repulse** had been sunk by Admiral Ozawa's carrier planes in the China Sea. These two warships had been rushed to the area to assist the British Forces on Singapore.

The British suffered a great loss in their defeat at Singapore. The opposition in the Philippines had also been soundly defeated by the Japanese. The Dutch Naval Units and the US Asiatic Fleet had been no match for Japan. The Pacific was rapidly becoming a Japanese 'Lake'.

Allied strategy was directed at building up a defensive force of US Army and Australian Army and Royal Australian Air Forces in the south and east of the Australian Territory of New Guinea. This area was just north of Australia across the Great Barrier Reef.

General Hideki Tojo, who was the Prime Minister of Japan at the time, had warned Australia and New Zealand, by radio, that they soon might "suffer the same fate as the Dutch East Indies." To carry out this threat Japanese Forces left their powerful Base at Rabaul, located on New Britain Island. This Island lay some distance to the north of the southern tip of New Guinea. The Japanese launched a two-pronged attack. One arm was an amphibious assault against Port Moresby on the southern side of the eastern tip of New Guinea, which was held by Australian Forces. A second arm of the assault was aimed at Tulagi in the Southern Solomon's chain of island. This island was just across Savo Sound from the island of Guadalcanal.

The enemies aim was three fold: 1.To establish control of all of the Solomon Islands. 2. To establish a seaplane base at Tulagi, after capturing it. Four motored seaplanes would be used for long range sea searches. 3. To occupy Port Moresby, and to build an airstrip Japanese planes could use to start bombing northern Australia as a prelude to invasion.

To accomplish these goals Japan sent the following:

A Carrier Striking Force to invade Australia
Composed of the following:
Two of the six Big Carriers that had bombed
Pearl Harbor the **Shokaku** and the **Zuikaku**;
Two Heavy Cruisers and six destroyers;
Two Oil Tankers

A Port Moresby Landing Force consisting of:
Transport consisting of a Minelayer with
Twelve Transports and Auxiliary craft
Attack Force consisting of:
A Light Cruiser escorted by six Destroyers
One Patrol Boat and an auxiliary craft

Close Support Force consisting of:
Four Heavy Cruisers

Close Cover Force consistng of:
Two Light Cruisers, A Seaplane Tender
Several Minelayers and Gunboats

For the Tulagi Operation the Force consisted of:
Two Destroyers;Two Minelayers; Two Transports
Various Auxiliary Craft.

Opposing this large Japanese Force to Invade Australia; the US had the following:

An Attack Group consisting of:
Cruisers: Minneapolis, New Orleans, Astoria,
Chester, and Portland
Destroyers: Phelps, Dewey, Farragut, Aylwin and
Monaghan

A Carrier Group consisting of:
Carriers: Yorktown and Lexington
Destroyers: Morris, Anderson, Hammann, Russel

A Support Group consisting of:

Australian Cruiser Hobart
US Cruiser: Chicago
Destroyers: Perkins and Walke

A Fueling Group consisting of:
Tankers: Neosho and Tippecanoe
Destroyers: Sims and Worden

THE CORAL SEA BATTLE BEGINS

At dawn of May 4, 1942 **Yorktown's** Air Group Five bombed Tulagi. The US attacking force consisted of 11 Torpedo Planes, 28 Dive Bombers and six Wildcat Fighters. 18 fighter planes were kept aboard for protection from Japanese planes.

The enemy forces were taken by surprise. A destroyer and 2 minesweepers were damaged. On a second strike a patrol boat was damaged and 2 seaplanes were destroyed. One US plane was shot down.

On a third strike in the afternoon 3 moored seaplanes were destroyed and an enemy destroyer was strafed. A later report revealed that the ship's captain was killed but with little damage to the destroyer. Two US planes were hit by antiaircraft fire but managed to land on Guadalcanal. Both pilots were rescued.

On May 5, 1942 the Japanese Striking Force entered the Coral Sea. The US Carrier Force meanwhile steamed toward the expected location of the enemy carriers. Neither Force Commander had any information concerning the other.

However, for the first time in the Pacific War a US fighter plane intercepted a Japanese Flying boat on patrol and shot it down. It was vectored to the enemy plane location by the use of shipboard radar.

On May 6, 1942 although the two fleets were only 70 miles apart neither force was aware of the other. The Japanese force was attacked by Army B-17's from Australian Airfields. The bombers dropped their bombs but were driven off the Japanese Zero fighter planes.

On May 7, 1942 both Forces launched major Air Strikes. The US was searching for the two enemy big carriers but instead located the Covering Force and sank the light carrier **Shoho**. This was the first Japanese Carrier sunk by aerial torpedoes and bombs. Also the first Japanese Zero was shot down by an American Pilot.

Late the same afternoon the Japanese launched 27 bombers. These planes were unable to locate the US Forces. All planes jettisoned their bombs and torpedoes. Landing on their carriers loaded with bombs and torpedoes was thought to be too dangerous to the Carriers. Inadvertantly the Japanese planes flew over the American Carrier force on the way back to their carriers. The US ships fired on them and American planes intercepted them and inflicted heavy losses.

On May 8, 1942 the Japanese Invasion Group retired from the area to leave the opposing Carrier Groups to fight it out. Each force had two carriers and 200 aircraft each. Scout planes from both forces located the opposing carriers about the same time.

At 10:57 (am) dive bombers and torpedo bombers from the US carriers attacked the **Shokaku.** They were attacked by **Zeros** in bad weather. One US dive bomber hit the enemy carrier with a 1000 lb. bomb. Another dive bomber hit the same carrier with another 1000 lb. bomb. These bombs caused extensive damage and ignited fires. A third SBD plane hit the same carrier with another 1000 lb. bomb. At this point the **Shokaku** retired from the area. She transferred her remaining planes to the **Zuikaku.** Meanwhile the **Zuikaku** hid in a rain storm and was not attacked by US planes.

One of the enemy search planes hid in the clouds and shadowed the US carriers and guided the enemy attacking aircraft to their targets. The **Lexington** tried to avoid multiple torpedoes in the water, but at 11:20 (am) she received two torpedo hits. Four Japanese torpedo planes attacked the **Yorktown** with torpedoes, but failed to hit her.

After the enemy torpedo planes finished their attacks, the enemy dive bomber began their attacks. Although the US Wildcats tried to fend them off, the **Lexington** suffered two bomb hits and numerous near misses.

Enemy dive bombers attacked the **Yorktown.** The **Yorktown** was able to avoid all but one bomb. This 250 kg bomb struck the center of the flight deck forward of the middle elevator rendering it inoperative. Several near misses caused damage below the waterline. Numerous dogfights erupted above the carriers throughout the attacks.

After the two enemy carriers retired from the scene the two US carriers were still able to make 24 knots and recover aircraft despite damage to the flight decks.

Aboard the **Lexington**, leaking gas caused an enormous explosion at 12:47 (pm) killing 25 men. Two more explosions wracked her. Things rapidly deteriorated and communications were crippled. Loss of steering control caused other problems. Fire main pressure dropped making it difficult to fight fires aboard. Soon more explosions wracked the hull.

At 17.07 (pm) the order to abandon ships was given. Weather conditions were ideal with a calm sea and at least 92% of the crew was rescued. A number of crew members who were trapped below deck, went down with the ship.

Five torpedoes were fired by the US destroyer **Phelps** while trying to sink the **Lexington**. The **Lexington** finally sank at 19:52 (pm).

As a result of the battle Japan gave up on the attempt to invade Australia and suffered her first major strategic defeat of the Pacific War.

During the Battle Japanese aircraft found the US destroyer **Sims** and sank it while damaging the US Oiler **Neosho.** After this battle ended Japan never again threatened to invade Australia by sea.

Meanwhile the **Yorktown**, although severely damaged, left the area with her escorting ships. She was able to reach Pearl Harbor under her own power. 72 hours later, after hasty repairs, she sailed to join the **Enterprise** and **Hornet** in the Battle of Midway.

Note: If the enemy invasion force had not been turned back and Australia would have been invaded; the invasion of New Zealand would have followed. In that case the War would have followed a completely different direction and the Helena would not have taken part in a naval battle in Kula Gulf.

Mindset of the Japanese concerning Midway

To the Americans, any President is just another citizen who has been voted into office for a specified term. While in the office he wields certain powers and has certain responsibilities. When his term of office is over the individual, whoever he may be, returns to civilian life just like he did before assuming the office of President.

With the Japanese the situation was completely different. Their ruler was the Emperor and he was in the office for life. This Emperor Hirohito, or Showa, was literally worshipped by all Japanese citizens. Whatever he said was law to them.

The B-25 bombing raid on Tokyo to the Japanese placed this ruler in danger and could not go unanswered.

Immediately the Japanese High Command set in motion retaliatory action.

The Higher Up Officers in the Japanese Air force knew the maximum range of a B-25, even when equipped with additional fuel tanks. According to their thinking, they could not grasp where the bombers came from. They did know that the American planes came from the south, but to their thinking there wasn't any land mass the American planes could have come from except the Island of Midway. To their way of thinking there was no way the planes could have flown that far. Although they had no idea how the Hated Yankees had done it they would make them pay for it. It never dawned on them that any one could be crazy enough to try and take off of a carrier deck in and army bomber.

117

THE BATTLE OF MIDWAY ISLAND

With this mental set, plans were made and action taken to send a mighty fleet to invade and hold the US held Island of Midway.

The fleet that Japan sent, up to that time, was the mightiest fleet ever to be sent to sea. Yamamoto (the architect of the Pearl Harbor Attack), the head of the Japanese military, had **Yamato** as his flagship. Yamato along with **Musashi** was one of the two world's mightiest battleships, as well as the newest. It mounted 18 inch guns.

The center pieces of this mammoth fleet were the remaining four carriers from the six that had participated in the Pearl Harbor Attack. These carriers were the **Akagi, Kaga**, **Horyu** and the **Soryu**. Escorting these four ships were as follows:

1. 11 battleships
2. 9 cruisers
3. 16 submarines
4. 49 destroyers
5. Plus a large variety of other supporting vessels.
6. 272 carrier planes of various types

A Photo of USS Yorktown after being bombed by
enemy aircraft at the Battle of Midway Island.

ON THE US SIDE

The Commander of the US Carrier Task Force was Admiral Nimitz, who remained in Pearl Harbor. The Carrier Task Force was under the command of Admiral Fletcher. Admiral Halsey was ill and had been replaced by Admiral Spruance. Admiral Spruance basically commanded the battle for the US side. There were three carriers; the **Enterprise, Yorktown** and **Hornet.** The number of carrier Planes was over 200.

The Battle of Midway was a major naval battle and turned out to be the most important battle of the Pacific War.

The Battle lasted from June 4 to June 7, 1942. This was only about a month after the Coral Sea battle, which was the first naval battle between carrier planes. Japan had captured Wake Island five months earlier. It happened six months after the attack on Pearl Harbor.

In the battle Japan lost all four carriers with most of their pilots, planes and crews. It was estimated that at least 200 carrier pilots were lost by Japan.

The US on the other hand lost the carrier **Yorktown.** The advantage the US had was that with its much larger Industrial Complex it was able to replace ships, planes etc. quicker than could Japan. By the year 1942 the US was in the third year of a massive warship building program.

The defeat at Midway set the Japanese back and in a rather short period of time the US forces were able to take the Offensive.

The Battle of Midway led directly to the enemies starting to build an airstrip on the Island of Guadalcanal. Their plan was to use this airstrip to allow land based planes to operate and extend Japan's area of conquest in the Pacific.

The enemies attempt to invade and hold the Solomon Islands and the air field at Guadalcanal led directly to the loss of the Helena in Kula Gulf.

THE BATTLE FOR THE SOLOMON ISLANDS

In July of 1942 a US plane on reconnaissance noticed enemy activity on the islands of Guadalcanal and Tulagi. Tulagi was across Savo Sound from Guadalcanal. It appeared that the Japanese were starting to grub out an airstrip on the north shore of Guadalcanal.

Since this could not be permitted, because of the land based planes that would operate from there; plans were made.

Marines were landed on Guadalcanal and Tulagi on August 8, 1942.

Almost instantly, after the Marine landings, the enemy reacted by sending planes down to attack the US Forces.

An enemy transport was sent at night to reinforce the troops on Guadalcanal. Enroute, the transport was sunk by the **US submarine S-38**. 500 men went down with the Transport.

On August 7 twenty seven enemy bombers attacked, escorted by 18 fighter planes, but achieved little success. 5 bombers were shot down.

The next day 27 enemy bombers loaded with torpedoes, and escorted by 15 Zero Fighters, attacked the Landing Force. One torpedo hit the US destroyer **Jarvis** in the bow. The transport **George F. Elliot** was struck by a plane crashing into it and setting it on fire. In the attack Japan lost 17 bombers and 2 fighters. Most of the planes were shot down by anti-aircraft guns aboard the ships.

The **Elliot** later sank; while the destroyers **Jarvis** and **Mugford**, though damaged, were able to sail for the Rear Base. However, the **Jarvis** encountered enemy planes on the way. She was attacked and sunk with the loss of all of her crew (Navy lingo 'hands').

NAVAL BATTLE OF SAVO ISLAND

The Japanese Forces at Rabaul launched another attempt to drive the marines into the sea. In this effort the Night Naval Battle of Savo Island occurred on August 9.

In this battle the Japanese dispatched 7 cruisers and 1 destroyer.

Although the US Forces were more numerous and powerful; errors in judgment by the US Commander, contributed to the worst disaster at Arms on the Sea for the US Navy.

The rout of the US Forces resulted in the sinking of the heavy cruisers **Astoria**, **Quincy**, **Vincennes** and the Australian cruiser **Canberra**.

One US cruiser was also damaged and 2 destroyers were damaged. 1,077 US military personnel were killed

In this Fiasco at sea Japan suffered only 3 cruisers moderately damaged and 58 killed.

A Photo of the Carrier Wasp after being torpedoed by a Japanese submarine.

SINKING OF THE CARRIER WASP

While the battle for Guadalcanal raged the US Carrier **Wasp** was sunk on September 15. The **Wasp** with her escorts was supporting the Marine landings. An enemy submarine fired several torpedoes, which resulted in the sinking of the **Wasp**.

The Naval Battle of the Eastern Solomon's

The Naval Battle of the Eastern Solomon's took place the night of August 24, 1942.

The Japanese Imperial Army Staff had failed to realize the strength of the Marine Landing. It was at this time that the enemy stood the best chance of driving the Marines off Guadalcanal. The American carriers had been withdrawn from the Landing Area for refueling.

The next attempt at reinforcing the Guadalcanal garrison consisted of 900 men, a detachment of the Japanese 28th Infantry Division. These troops were loaded aboard six fast destroyers. They were unloaded at Guadalcanal without incident.

In the subsequent fighting, at the Battle of the Tenaru River with the marines, 800 of the enemy were killed.

One problem the enemy had was the disagreement between the Army commanders and the Naval commanders. The Army preferred to concentrate their efforts on crossing the Owens Stanley Mountains on New Guinea and capturing Port Moresby. This Port would then be a stepping stone to the invasion of northern Australia.

This military adventure was thwarted by the Australian armies in the subsequent fighting. The Japanese were driven back.

Belatedly the Japanese planned a major effort to drive the Marines off Guadalcanal. Their Task Force consisted of two big carriers and one small carrier. These ships were escorted by two heavy cruisers and several destroyers. Another group of ships consisting of five heavy cruisers with their destroyer escort and a seaplane tender was ordered to the base at Truk Islands. Yamamoto meanwhile sailed aboard his flagship **Yamato**, with its escorts.

On the other side, the American Commanders had no information as the size of the enemy formation, or the intent of its mission. They did know that one of the six big carriers had been severely damaged at the Battle of the Coral Sea. But, they had no information that either of the two big carriers had been repaired and were available to reenter the Pacific War.

In this new attempt a contingent of 1500 army men were sent to Guadalcanal. After the enemies defeat at the Tenaru River this group was directed to land at Guadalcanal.

The plan was that the new troops would break through the marine lines and their planes would land at the new field at Guadalcanal.

Opposing this Force the US had the carriers **Saratoga**, **Enterprise** and **Wasp** escorted by the battleship **North Carolina**, seven cruisers and eighteen destroyers. This was a far cry from the few vessels the US had at the Battle for Midway Island in June.

The information as to the location of the enemy Force was sketchy. It was though that the enemy was heading for Truk, when it actually was enroute to Guadalcanal, and was only two days away by sea. The Japanese Force was under Radio Silence.

The Search planes from both sides were searching for the opposing Force. The US had planes from Henderson Field operating out of the mud there. There were also PBY sea planes and B-17 bombers from Espiritu plus six more PBYs from the nearby island of Ndeni. At around 09:50 (am) on the 23rd August a US plane made contact with Tanaka's Reinforcement Group.

At 02:00 on August 24 Light carrier **Ryujo** escorted by heavy cruiser Tone and two destroyers headed south at 24 knots. The mission was two fold. First in importance was to strike at Henderson Field. Second in importance was to cover the trailing convoy.

At 09:20 a flying boat PBY from Ndeni sighted **Ryujo** and made their report by radio. A second sighting of Kondo's Advance Force was made and the Vanguard Force under Abe.

With the two reports in hand Admiral Fletcher ordered **Saratoga** to launch sixteen SBD's and seven TBF's. The pilots were ordered to search out to 250 nautical miles.

At 14:45 (pm) the **Saratoga** launched 31 dive bombers and 6 torpedo planes. There were also eleven dive bombers and their fighter escorts from Henderson Field. Eight fighter aircraft and 3 torpedo aircraft were kept aboard as protection of the carrier.

During the night Henderson Field was shelled by the Japanese destroyer **Kagero**.

A B-17 from Espiritu had already bombed **Ryujo** but was unsuccessful

125

in getting a bomb hit. Her missing combat air patrol left her vulnerable to attack.

In the air attack that followed **Ryujo** experienced three bomb hits and one torpedo hit. **Ryujo** sank at 20:00 hours.

Belatedly Admiral Fletcher realized that the enemy had the two big carriers. He tried to contact his previously launched strike to try and recall them. Unfortunately he was unable to do so.

By this time the Japanese Admiral Nagumo knew where the American carriers were. A Chikuma float plane had reported the sighting.

Enemy planes were picked up on radar at 16:00 (pm) at a distance of 85 nautical miles flying at 12,000 feet. Wildcat fighters from the carrier were launched and went up after the attacking bombers. Losses on both sides were severe. At 16:42 (pm) hours the carrier crews knew the enemy planes were overhead. **Enterprise** was able to avoid 22 of the 25 attacking planes. However, the remaining three planes achieved bomb hits. The damage from the bombs was contained and **Enterprise** was still able to make 24 knots.

Unfortunately one bomb caused a loss of steering power for an extended period of time. During this time a second wave of enemy aircraft missed **Enterprise** and flew on past her.

Steering control was finally established and **Enterprise** and her escorts sailed for Espritu and reached there safely.

Meanwhile planes from the American found them and attacked. Eight SBDs from Henderson bombed the light cruiser **Jintsu**. The bombs knocked out two guns, killing many of the crew and rendering Tanaka unconscious. A second **Enterprise** plane bombed the transport **Kinryu Maru**. The freighter was carrying much needed ammunition for Guadalcanal.

Army B-17 planes found and bombed destroyer **Mutsuki** and the **transport**, and sank them both.

Enterprise sailed for Pearl Harbor for repairs. **Ryujo** had been sunk and the two big carriers, **Shokaku** and **Zuikaku** had received heavy damage, and were out of the war for an extended period of time.

The Americans had received a chance to gather their breath.

THE NAVAL BATTLE OF CAPE ESPERANCE

This was the first naval battle that the Light Cruiser Helena was involved in.

This naval battle occurred on the night of October 11/12/1942.

During the month of September the enemy was able to operate unmolested by US Forces. The **Wasp** had been sunk by submarine torpedoes. The **Saratoga** had also been torpedoed along with the new battleship **North Carolina**. **Enterprise's** flight deck was in need of repairs, due to three bomb hits. The only carrier available at this time was **Hornet**.

Frequent destroyer-transports delivered supplies to Guadalcanal. There was a growing feeling that Guadalcanal could not be held. Instead it was felt that the marines should be transferred to the nearby island of Ndeni.

Both sides landed reinforcements on Guadalcanal. The Japanese landed 22,000 men equipped with heavy artillery.

At this stage the enemy sent its three remaining heavy cruisers which were screened by destroyers to bombard Henderson Field.

Opposing this force was a US counter force consisting of four cruisers and five destroyers. This force sailed undetected for Guadalcanal to prevent the bombardment of the marines.

The enemy force advanced in a T formation with destroyers on the flagships flanks. The **Aoba**, **Furutaka** and **Kinugasa** were in line behind the flagship.

Meanwhile the US force sailed directly north until almost the same latitude of Cape Esperance. This Cape was off the western tip of Guadalcanal.

This naval battles was the third of five major naval engagements in this campaign,

On October 11 four US cruisers and five destroyers met Japanese Admiral Goto's force. One Japanese cruiser was sunk and heavily damaged a second cruiser. An enemy destroyer was also sunk.Goto was mortally wounded. The remaining Japanese ships retired.

Other Naval Battles

The Naval Battle of Santa Cruz was fought on October 26.

The Naval Battle of Tassafaranga occurred on November 3.

Ten days later on November 13 the First Naval Battle of Guadalcanal was fought.

Two nights later, on November 15, the Second Naval Battle of Guadalcanal was also fought.

From the middle of November until February of 1943 there was a lull in the fighting on the sea. Both sides were running short of warships. On the beach the two opposing Forces were exhausted.

On February 7 the enemy sent 198 planes to bomb the marines and any US ships in the vicinity of Guadalcanal.

The Japanese Officers in charge at Rabaul, began to realize that they could no longer support their troops on Guadalcanal. These Forces were withdrawn without incident and the fight moved up to the Island of New Georgia.

As a prelude to the US Landing on New Georgia a landing was made on a nearby Island. This Island was Rendova and the landing was made on July 4.

Two days later on July 6, 1943 a second US landing was made at night at Rice Anchorage located on the north shore of New Georgia. The Main enemy Base on New Georgia was located at Munda on the south shore.

In support of the New Georgia Operation the night time Naval Engagement occurred on July 13 in the Battle of Kolombangara.

It was at this time that the Helena was sunk in Kula Gulf.

Naval Ships that were Lost in the Pacific in World War II prior to the Battle of Kula Gulf where the Helena was sunk.

One of the main reasons for the **Helena** being in that battle was because so many US ships had been lost in the previous fighting at sea. *A listing of the ships lost follows:*

Battleships:

1. USS **Arizona** (BB39) was sunk by Japanese aerial bombs in the attack on Pearl Harbor on December 7,1941. A bomb penetrated a magazine and virtually destroyed the ship and killed most of the crew.
2. USS **Oklahoma** (B37) was torpedoed and capsized in the Pearl Harbor attack.
3. Various other battleships were heavily damaged in the Pearl Harbor attack and required extensive repairs in US Navy Yards prior to returning to duty.

Carriers:

1. USS **Langley** ( )
2. The US Carrier **Lexington** (CV3) was torpedoed by Japanese carrier aircraft in the Battle of the Coral Sea and sank. The attempted invasion of Japanese forces to invade northern Australia was turned back.
3. The carrier **Yorktown** (CV5) was heavily damaged by enemy carrier dive bombers in the Battle of the Coral Sea. She was able to return to Pearl Harbor under her own power for emergency repairs. 72 hours after repairs were started she sailed to join the carriers **Enterprise** and **Hornet** at the Battle of Midway Island. She was sunk by torpedoes from the **Japanese Submarine I-126** after suffering previous damage. She sank on June 7, 1942.
4. The US carrier **Hornet** (CV8) was sunk by being torpedoed by Japanese Aircraft during the Battle of Santa Cruz in the Solomon Chain of Island campaign. The sinking occurred on October 26,1942.
5. An aside: The carrier USS **Ranger** () never served in the Pacific except in the Training of Night Fighter Pilots.
6. The USS **Saratoga** ( ) was torpedoed twice during the Solomon's Campaign and was never actually in combat but

spent many months is Dry Dock for repairs. She was able to sail under her own power to the repair facilities.

Heavy Cruisers:

1. The first heavy cruiser sunk in the Pacific War was the USS **Houston** (CA30) on March 21, 1942. She was sunk by gunfire and torpedoes from Japanese naval forces in Sunda Straits in the Netherlands East Indies. She was a part of a joint Task Force including Dutch vessels.

2. Three US heavy cruisers were sunk in a night time attack off Savo Island in the Solomon Islands on August 9, 1942.The 3 heavy cruisers were the USS **Astoria** (CA34); the USS **Quincy** (CA39) and the USS **Vincennes** (CA 44). In the same action an Australian heavy cruiser was also sunk. The enemy cruiser force (totaled 7) and 1 destroyer escorting the cruisers suffered only minor damage. It was the worst US defeat at sea in the history of the United States Navy.

3. The last Heavy Cruiser sunk prior to the sinking of the USS **Helena** was the USS Northampton (CA 26). She was struck by a torpedo from the **Japanese submarine Oyashio** during the Battle of Tassafaronga and sank on December 1,1942.

4. Various other heavy cruiser suffered extensive damage in the night time battles that erupted in the Slot in the earlier days of the Solomons Campaign to drive the Japanese out of the Solomon Islands.

Light Cruisers:

1.A light cruiser sunk in the Solomons Campaign was the USS **Atlanta** (CL 51).She was damaged by gunfire from enemy warships during the night time naval battle of Guadalcanal. She was scuttled off Lunga Point.

Destroyers:

1. The USS **Sims**(DD 409) was sunk on May 7, 1942 during the Battle of the Coral Sea.

2. The USS **Hammann** (DD 412) was torpedoed by the Japanese submarine I-168 northeast of Midway Island on June 6, 1942 and sunk.

3. The USS **Jarvis** (DD 393) was sunk by Japanese aircraft south of Guadalcanal on August 9, 1942.
4. The USS **Meredith** (DD 434) was sunk by Japanese aircraft near Cristobal on October 15, 1942.
5. The USS **O'Brien** was torpedoed September 15, 1942 by the Japanese submarine I-15 north of Espritu Santo, New Hebrides Islands. After being torpedoed she foundered off Samoa en route to base on October 18,1942.
6. The USS **Porter** (DD 356) was torpedoed and sunk by the Japanese submarine I-21 near Santa Cruz Islands located east of the Solomon Islands on October 26, 1942.
7. The USS **Cushing** (DD 376) was sunk by gunfire off Savo Island on November 13, 1942.
8. The USS **Laffey** (DD 459) was sunk by gunfire from the Japanese battleship **Hiei** off Savo on November 13, 1942. She was sunk in the same battle as the **Cushing** and **Monssen**.
9. The USS **Walke** (DD 416) was sunk by gunfire and torpedoes from enemy warships off Savo on November 14, 1942.
10. The USS **Monssen** (DD 436) was sunk by gunfire off Savo on November 13,1942.
11. The USS **Aaron Ward** (DD 483) was sunk after being bombed by Japanese aircraft off

Tagoma Point on April 7, 1943.

It was because of the loss of all of the above ships that resulted in the Helena being involved in the Kula Gulf night time naval action. There were not many US or Japanese ships at that point in the War remaining to continue carrying on the fight in the Solomon's Islands.

Although the US had a massive warship building program underway in the States those new ships were still in various stages of construction. Wars are fought with what one has not what will be available in the future.

Four months later after the enemy Forces on New Georgia had been defeated or driven off the island the war moved up to the Island of Bougainville. A landing there at Empress Augusta Bay was made at night on November 11.

On February 13, 1944 a landing was made at Green Islands. This

Landing was part of the Operation to isolate the main Enemy Base that was located at Rabaul on the northern tip of the Island of New Britain.

Five destroyers from Destroyer Squadron bombarded the harbor at Rabaul on the night of February 18.

A Second Bombardment was made on February 25 in daylight on the coast of the island of Kavieng.

This final Operation officially ended the Struggle for the Solomon Islands. All Enemy Forces had either been killed; driven off the islands or isolated, and left to starve as their supply routes had been severed.

The War at sea then moved to the North.

A Formidable Foe

It might have been beneficial if the American men who fought the Solomon's Campaign had had an inking of the mental set of the enemy, which they did not have.

Between the 9th and 12th century Japan was a medieval country. At that time there was group of Samurai Warriors that lived by the Code of Bushido. It is reported that this code was similar to the age of chivalry of the European Knights. Emphasis was placed on purity, modesty, frugality, justice, sense of shame (to a very high degree), refined manners, honor and affection.

The code of Bushido arose from out of Buddhism, Zen, Confucianism and Shintoism. It was a amalgamation of all of the religions that led to Bushido. It was from all of this that Bushido got its beliefs concerning danger and death. The Samaurai were virtually fearless because of their Buddhism teachings. It was their belief that after death they would be reincarnated and live again on earth. The Samaurai used the Zen teachings to drive out fear, unsteadiness and to ultimately make mistakes. It was thought that any kind of weakness could result in their death and this weakness was to be avoided at all costs.

Another facet of Japanese religious life was Shintoism which involved loyalty and patriotism. It also includes ancestor-worship. The untimate result was it ascribed a god-like reverence to the Emperor. To the Samaurai the Emperor was the embodiment of Heaven here on earth. As a result of this mind set the Samauri pledged themselves to the Emperor for life. To them their homeland was the sacred abode of the gods which included the spirits of their forefathers.

Over a long period of time the average Japanese warrior adopted the code of the Samurai which basically from the American way of thinking would be expressed as, "Death before dishonor".

Almost from birth they were indoctrinated with the virtues of reckless bravery, a fierce family pride and selflessness almost senseless devotion to the master.

This train of thought led inevitably to the ritual of Seppuku. To atone for perceived failings to Save Face the individual was required to commit suicide in a particular custom. To the English speaking world the ritual is known as Harakiri.

In conformance with this ritual the individual used a particular ceremonial knife. While in a sitting position, and wearing a ceremonial robe, the knife was plunged into the abdomen, and then used to slice across the abdomen. The individual was forbidden by the code to show any evidence of the intense pain experienced by either a grimace or any kind of sound.

After finishing the cutting motion the individual who must have been in excruciating pain then was required to stretch out the neck. An assistant would then decapitate the individuals head from the body.

Although it is almost impossible for an occidental, or westerner, to grasp this form of atonement; to the Japanese it was very real.

The main point of the act was to restore one's honor.

If the marines on Guadalcanal, as well on other islands had, had any inkling as to the mind set of their foe they would have been more able to grasp their actions in battle.

During one very tense part of the Guadalcanal Japanese soldiers by the hundreds charged the marine lines screaming as they ran. The marine machine guns and rifles cut them down but they would regroup and charge the marines again and again under almost a thousand of them lay dead

At this point the Japanese commander in charge of these troops committed Suppuku because he felt he had failed the Emperor, by not being able to break through the marine lines.

In sense it was this failure to destroy the Marines that led eventually to the Japanese abandonment of Guadalcanal and regrouping further up the Solomon's Chain. This regrouping was on the island of New Georgia and it was in this area that the battles of Kula Gulf were fought.

THE CRUISER HELENA ENTERS THE PACIFIC WAR

After returning to the Pacific Area when repairs at Mare Island had been completed, she escorted a detachment of Sea Bees (Navy construction personnel) in 1942 to the South Pacific. Also with her was an aircraft carrier ferrying planes.

She made two trips by sea between Espiritu Santo (The Navy Forward Base for the Solomon's Campaign) where the Battle for the airfield at Guadalcanal was just beginning to take shape. After completing these missions she was assigned to A Task Force centered around the carrier USS **Wasp.**

The **Wasp** Task Force steamed at some distance from six transports carrying Marine reinforcements for Guadalcanal. On September 15, 1942 at about mid-afternoon the **Wasp** suffered hits by three torpedoes fired from an undetected enemy submarine. In a matter of moments she became a raging inferno with her aviation fuel on fire and exploding magazines.

Meanwhile during the sinking **Helena** rescued 400 of the **Wasp's** officers and crew. The men rescued were taken to Espiritu.

Helena's next action occurred near Rennel Island (A small island some distance north and west of Guadalcanal). Attacks by US planes from the new airfield at Guadalcanal (Henderson field) had slowed down the Tokyo Express (Japanese destroyers carrying supplies and reinforcements for Guadalcanal).

On October 11, 1942 the Japanese put everything they could deliver against the Henderson Field airstrip. The enemies hope was to neutralize any US air operations long enough to bring in heavy enemy troop reinforcements during the night. By 18:10 pm the enemy fleet was less than 100 miles from Savo Island (A small island near Guadalcanal on the west).

The **Helena** in the US Task Force was the first to pick up the enemy formation on radar and also the first US ship to open fire. Firing began at 23:46 pm. When the firing by the US ships had ceased in the **Naval Battle of Cape Esperance** in Savo Sound (Iron Bottom Bay as named by the sailors who fought there) the enemy cruiser **Furutaka** and the enemy destroyer **Fubuki** were both sunk. The Japanese ships **Aoba**, **Kinugase** and **Hatsuyuki** all retired with various degrees of damage.

On the night of October 20 **Helena** came under attack while patrolling between Espiritu Santo and San Cristobal. Several torpedoes exploded near her but she did not sustain any damage from them.

When the First Naval Battle of Guadalcanal took place **Helena** was assigned the task of escorting a supply group of ships from Espiritu to Guadalcanal. Rendezvous was made with the transport convoy off San Cristobal on November 11. San Cristobal is a large island just south of Guadalcanal. It did not enter into the Guadalcanal campaign. The convoy was brought through safely. Word from the Coast Watchers was received during the afternoon of November 12, indicating that "enemy aircraft were approaching the landing area." Unloading operations were suspended and all ships stood out and formed up into a defensive formation awaiting the arrival of the enemy planes. The force was superbly handled during the air attack. The antiaircraft firing from the US ships broke up the attack. Damage to two ships was suffered. **Helena** emerged from the air attack without any damage. The task force shot down eight of the attacking enemy force. The action lasted eight minutes.

Unloading operations were resumed while increasing reports continued to come in from patrolling aircraft about continued enemy operations up the Slot. The ominous nature of the reports arose because there were no transports reported in the enemy formation. It became increasing evident that the enemy task force was an offensive one.

Meanwhile **Helena** continued steaming with the transports away from the Guadalcanal Landing Site. After a period of time the formation was ordered to reverse course to return to Guadalcanal.

On the night of November 13 a Friday **Helena's** radar picked up the enemy formation. The tropical night was lit up by the flashes from the big guns from both the Japanese and Americans.

Helena sustained only minor damage to her superstructure during the action. However when daylight arrived it presented a grisly scene in Iron Bottom Bay. The weaker US force that consisted of cruisers and destroyers had prevented a much more powerful enemy force of battleships, cruisers and destroyers from bombarding Henderson Field. But stopping the bombardment had been at a heavy cost to both sides. If the bombardment had succeeded it would have been a disaster for the Marines on the island.

During the engagement the Commanding Officer of the **Helena** had been killed and the command shifted to another Captain. He was in command upon the withdrawal of the **Helena** and the other surviving ships. One of the US ships that had been sunk was the USS **Juneau**. The new commander of the **Helena** believed that the danger from enemy submarines was too great for the **Helena** to delay trying to rescue any survivors of the **Juneau** and left the area without searching. It was later found that at least a hundred men of the **Juneau** had survived. However they all died from exposure waiting for rescue that never came. When this information became available the new commander of the **Helena** was relieved from command.

During January of 1943 **Helena** in company with other ship units engaged in several bombardments of Japanese positions located on the island of New Georgia. The main enemy concentrations located at Munda and Vila Stanmore were extensively shelled. **Helena** participated in this shelling. The bombardments leveled vital concentrations of enemy supplies and gun emplacements.

Helena continued to support operations in the Guadalcanal through the month of February. She was involved in patrol and escort duties. One of her float planes (Biplanes equipped with pontoons that were carried aboard) contributed to the sinking of the enemy **sub RO-102** on February 1, 1943.

Sinking of the Helena in Kula Gulf

Helena then sailed to a navy yard in Sydney, Australia. After completion of work there she returned to Espiritu and from there to New Georgia in March to participate in the bombardments. These bombardments were in support of the ground troops. These bombardments were a prelude to invasion. Rice Anchorage was the first site on New Georgia for a landing at night. The cruiser task force screened the initial landing party.

It was on July 4 just before midnight that **Helena** opened up on her last shore bombardment.

Finding the river mouth in the darkness and inclement weather presented some difficulties. However, with the assistance of Natives the landing was made successfully. This landing was completed by dawn of the following day. On the afternoon of July 5 the ships were alerted that the Tokyo Express was ready to landing more reinforcement troops. The US Force, which included the **Helena,** turned to meet the enemy and prevent the landing.

As midnight on July 5 arrived the **Helena's** group of ships was off the northwest corner of the island of New Georgia. The force consisted of three cruisers and four destroyers. Facing the US force was an enemy force consisting of three groups of Japanese destroyers totaling ten ships in all. Four of the enemy destroyers left the formation to accomplish their mission of landing troops.

At 01:57 am **Helena** opened fire with her big guns and began shelling the enemy formation. Her main battery of six inch guns fired on one large enemy ship sinking it. Meanwhile, her secondary batteries fired on an enemy destroyer sinking it also. A second enemy destroyer was then taken under fire resulting in its sinking also. Both main and secondary batteries had shifted to new targets and were believed to have inflicted great damage on them. It was believed later that in all the enemy formation had suffered nine ships sunk.

Unfortunately **Helena** ran out of flashless powder for its six inch guns.

The Captain unwisely ordered that firing be continued with flash type powder. This unwise decision led to the end of **Helena.** Unfortunately the flashes from Helena's guns provided two of the enemy destroyers with a perfect target.

When **Helena's** guns began to light up the enemy destroyers used that as an aiming point. The enemy destroyers fired spreads of torpedoes at the flashes and turned away. Seven minutes after the torpedoes were fired **Helena** was hit by the first of three torpedoes. The first torpedo took off her bow which upended and continued to float. The next two torpedoes broke her in two and she went down rapidly.

The ship went down in only twenty minutes. Her crew abandoned ship in an orderly manner which tended to prevent more losses.

The bow of the **Helena,** which had broken off, now floated upright in the sea and a large number of the crew gathered around it. Unfortunately they were fired on while in the water.

After about a half hour later two of the destroyers that had screened the **Helena** arrived and began a rescue effort. That which followed is a tale of incredible valor.

The Captain of the **Helena** had previously been decorated for extraordinary heroism for actions he had taken while the Commanding Officer of a destroyer group.

He proceeded to direct the operation in a calm and efficient manner in the abandonment and subsequent rescue efforts. He conducted this operation from a small life raft. Prior to this he spent five hours in the oil-covered waters along with other members of the crew. He also spent ten more hours on a life raft before managing to reach one of the nearer islands.

Some members of the crew that were rescued stated that although the Captain had an offer to board one of the two destroyers that was rescuing crewmen from the water, but that he refused. He stated that he preferred to stay in the water with the rest of the crew in order to see to it that the men who could not be rescued immediately, at least reached shore safely.

At this point the two destroyers **Nickolas** (DD-449) and **Radford** (DD-446) began to rescue men from the sea. Each ship took as many aboard as they could accommodate and locate in the darkness.

As dawn arrived the two destroyers broke off their rescue efforts as they anticipated air attacks from enemy planes at the nearby enemy airfields. It was felt that if the ships were attacked, the sinkings would have made the situation much worse. Therefore the two ships retired to the harbor at

Tulagi at maximum speed. At Tulagi all of those rescued were debarked and those that needed medical help were turned over to the medical staffs on the beach. The two ships had been forced to leave approximately 275 crewmen in the waters around the sunken ship.

However, before leaving the battle area the motor whaleboats from both ships were lowered in the water. A small Flotilla consisting of three whaleboats were manned with voluntary crews. Each boat towed a life raft from one of the destroyers. These three boats were only able to take aboard 88 men and carried them to a small island about 7 miles from Rice Anchorage. It took an all day laborious passage to accomplish this.

Two destroyers the Gwin (DD-433) and the Woodworth (DD-460) departed Tulagi just before dusk and after steaming at full power of 31 knots arrived at the above location and rescued the 88 crewmen who had reached this island.

Comment: This writer was a Signal Watch Supervisor on one of the destroyers that effected this rescue.

However, there was still a second group in the water, amounting in number to about 200, near the bow of the **Helena.** It was serving as their life raft but it too was slowly sinking.

The situation appeared to be hopeless until a Navy Liberator plane spotted the men in the water and dropped lifejackets and four rubber lifeboats in the water nearby.

The wounded were then place in the rubber lifeboats, while the able-bodied men surrounded the boats and did their best to propel them to Kolombangara. Unfortunately winds and adverse currents carried them further into enemy waters. Through the torturous day that followed many of the wounded died for lack of medical help.

American search planes combing the area failed to spot the small group and the island faded away to leeward. Another night passed and in the morning the island of Vella Lavella loomed dead ahead. Reaching the beach there seemed to be there only hope for survival. By dawn all surviving members of the small group managed to safely land on the island.

At the place that they landed were two Coastwatcher and a number of loyal friendly natives. They cared for the men as best they could. The Coastwatchers had a radio and were in touch with Guadalcanal. News of the refugees was radioed to the Authorities at Guadalcanal.

Prior to landing on the island, a Major Kelly and five marines had been in the water for 30 hours. The men in the boats had been able to rig a jury rigged sail and with constant paddling had finally managed to reach shore. Some of the fortunate ones who reached shore stated that over the long hours they were in the water now and then one of the men would slip beneath the water and be gone.

During the long hours in the water a sack of potatoes from the sunken **Helena** had drifted nearby. The men found that chewing on one of the potatoes helped ease their thirst. Fortunately for the men during their long hours in the water they were not bothered by sharks.

The ones who survived could hardly remember who they were. They were all covered with oil and were suffering from severe physical exhaustion and occasional mental relapses.

One of the boats had been able to reach Vella Lavella but the other boat had continued to drift.

The following day two officers on the second boat decided to swim for the shore on Vella Lavella. They were picked up by natives in an outrigger canoe about a mile out from the beach. The other boat finally made shore. Some of the men were almost naked or had on makeshift clothing. Fortunately even with the crude care they received their condition improved.

A day or so later a semi-permanent camp had been set up in the jungle. They were sheltered by giant Banyan trees from the searching eye of the enemy on ships or in planes. The wounded were put to bed in the house of a friendly Chinese. Medical supplies and emergency rations that had been collected from some of the ship's rafts which had drifted ashore, furnished food for the injured. The natives brought a daily supply of potatoes, tapioca, yams, papaws and other tropical food to the encampment.

With four cans of meat and native vegetable a stew was made twice daily and was the principle article at mealtime. Also five 25 lb. cans of coffee washed up on the beach.

The natives reported that Japanese patrols and scouting parties on Vella Lavella were searching for any sailors off the **Helena**. Also it was noted that enemy planes from Munda had been spotted flying overhead.

The thing uppermost in everyone's mind was the fear of being discovered and captured. To cope with this eventuality a guard was organized consisting of the five marines and a few of the able bodied sailors.

From the natives they were able to gather up seven old rifles, and a shotgun. The rifle was of Japanese make. Enough ammunition was scrounged up to provide a number of rounds per gun. Guards were posted nightly around the camp.

In addition the natives prowled the jungle to detect any enemy activity. It was reported that a small enemy patrol ventured too near the camp. The native quickly killed them all, probably without making any sound.

Communication was established with the main base at Tulagi and plans were made to rescue the survivors. Another small group from the **Helena** had made shore a short distance away.

Rescuing these men would be a bold and daring venture as it was right near the Enemies stronghold. The enemy was in control of Kolombangara and Vella Lavella and all the waters around them. Besides, there were no charts of the waters around either island that were available. The Solomon Islands were all uncharted. Any ships making the rescue would have to negotiate crooked and narrow channels in total darkness, with the risk of running aground.

To compound the problem all US ships were heavily involved in supporting landing operations that were being made on New Georgia and Rendova (a smaller nearby island). The rescue would have to be made at night as trying to do so in the day time would risk being attacked by enemy aircraft.

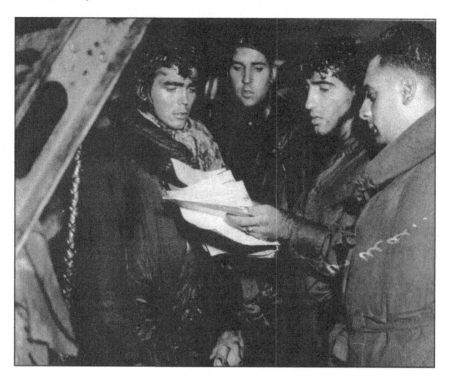

RESCUE OF THE SURVIVORS ON VELLA LAVELLA

The ships that were to perform the rescue consisted of the older world war I destroyers (four stackers) that would actually venture in to shore and bring the refugees aboard. These two destroyers were the **USS Dent** and the **USS Waters.**

Two groups of the newer 2100 ton destroyers would act as a screen. These destroyers would fend off any effort by the enemy to interfere with the rescue by sea. One escort group consisted of the destroyers **Taylor, Maury, Gridley** and the **Ellet.** The commander of this group was aboard the Taylor. Captain Thomas J.Ryan was the commander of the group. The outer screen of destroyers was the USS **Jenkins,** USS **O'Bannon** and the USS **Nicholas.** Captain McInerney was aboard the **Nicholas.**

The transports and their escort departed from Guadalcanal on July 15. The combined Force proceeded towards Vella Lavella, keeping the island of New Georgia (The main enemy base of Munda was on this island) to starboard (to the right). That part of the ocean area was familiar to the navigators up to the island of Rendova as the ships had been that far before. Beyond Banyetts Point the ocean area was unfamiliar. The sea, the islands and reefs there were also unfamiliar. The sky was clear and unclouded with a full moon in view. This made the sailing easier but also carried the increased risk of being detected.

Midnight approached and the rescue location was near. As the destroyers neared shore they decreased speed and proceeded slowly and cautiously for fear of shallow waters and reefs. The depth of water adjacent to the ships was determined by taking soundings. Soundings were where a line with a lead weight was lowered until the weight touched bottom. There were marks on the line that let the operator know how deep the water was at that point.

Although the individuals in charge of the ships had reason to believe that the ships were near the rendezvous area there was no sign in the inky darkness that this was true. The Commander was beginning to think something was remiss. However, at precisely at 02:00 am a blinking light was seen from the shore. One of the survivors was a signalman from the **Helena**. It was this individual who was sending a message by flashing light. A senior signalman on the lead destroyer informed the Captain that the flashing signal seemed to be reliable.

The two older destroyers ventured into as shallow a water as deemed safe, while the newer destroyers patrolled back and forth with their surface radars and underwater gear searching for any enemy activity.

The whaleboats of the two destroyers were lowered into the water and ventured to shore. They were guided first by the dim flashing light and then by voices by those on shore. After a period of time passed the boats began to return loaded with some of the refugees. Some of them were so weak they had to be lifted aboard. Others appeared to be in good health and got aboard unaided. They were all suffering from coral cuts and sore feet as they had abandoned their shoes in the sea. The few Marines ashore guarded the party until all were aboard the two destroyers. They were the last ones to board one of the whaleboats.

The two transport destroyers left the area, and proceeded down the coast of the island to the second rendezvous point where another small group of survivors awaited them. At 05:00 am the group of 61 men came aboard. By this time dawn was near and it was imperative that the destroyers depart the scene before any air patrols could detect them.

Previous to the start of the Rescue Operation the escorting group consisting of four destroyers left Tulagi later because they could travel faster. This force departed from Tulagi at mid-afternoon on July 16th. While off Kolombangara at about 11:00 pm they were sighted by a Japanese reconnaissance plane which shadowed them the rest of the night. The plane probably sighted the destroyers by their wake (a white streak in the sea).

The enemy planes continued to shadow the destroyers and dropped flares to illuminate them. Twice aerial bombs were dropped without inflicting any damage. Fortunately these planes concentrated on the covering force and were completely unaware of the older destroyers loaded with the survivors.

The Captain of the covering force abstained from tracking the planes by radar and firing on them as he was not willing to risk attracting the attention of any surface vessels that might be in the area.

The return trip to the Guadalcanal/Tulagi area was uneventful except that a number of enemy personnel were found in the water enroute. These men were from enemy ships sunk in the battle. A few were taken aboard as prisoner. A number of enemy personnel in the water, when offered rescue, declined, preferring to basically commit suicide by drowning in the sea. To them apparently to surrender was a matter of dishonor to the Emperor.

On the afternoon of July 17 the combined force reached the Tulagi area and the Survivors, who were wounded or still able bodied, were debarked.

And so the Rescue of the Helena Survivors came to an End. But, the Story of the Incredible Courage and Bravery of the Rescued and the Rescuers will live Forever in the Annals of the United States Navy.

Freemen must always stand as a bulwark against Evil wherever it may be.

God Bless America!